Contents and Foreword

Foreword

When first deciding to write a social history of Ashley Cross, I thought the finished book would be fairly short. The following pages, however, have proved me wrong - there is still much more information that could be researched, but I had to stop somewhere! I have, more or less, confined my research to the boundaries of the Conservation Area.

Every effort has been made to trace the owners of photographs, but unfortunately it has not always been possible.

Iris Morris

Contents ....

Opposite page shows
a section of an 1890 map, reproduced
by kind permission of Ordnance Survey

About the Author

Iris Morris

Moving to Parkstone from north London nearly 40 years ago
the author became very interested in local history, and was a regular contributor to
the Dorset Life magazine in the 1980's.

Her first book, 'The Llewellin Family of Upton House', was published in 1993.

Old Thyme Publishing
2nd Floor
Jonsen House
43 Commercial Road
Poole, Dorset BH14 0HU

ISBN 0 9520752 1 0

Editing - Phœnix 2, Lantern House, Woodfalls, Salisbury SP5 2NH

Typesetting and Design - Mellissa Fry, 4 Egdon Court, Dorchester Road, Upton, Poole, Dorset BH16 5NR

Print - Wilton Graphics, Salisbury, Wiltshire

A Snapshot

Ashley Cross is part of Parkstone, Poole in the county of Dorsetshire. It is an urban village lying beside the main A35 road between Poole and Bournemouth and despite the huge volume of daily traffic which passes through, albeit rather slowly at times, the area still retains its village atmosphere. There are several non-conformist churches, as well as the parish church, a library, pubs and restaurants, a variety of shops, a doctors' surgery, a village green and a railway station.

'Parkson' appears on Ralph **Treswell's** map of 1586 above the *'Mynes'*, which were probably the alum works opened by James **Blount**, **Lord Mountjoy**. The landscape then between Poole and Christchurch would have been of desolate heathland; and the area of Ashley Cross began to be developed in the early 1800's, more or less at the same time as was Bournemouth.

The land on which now stands the Central Hotel was bought at auction in 1807, and 1833 saw the consecration of the first St Peter's Church and the opening of St Peter's School. An 1844 Tithing Map of Great Canford shows that the oldest part of Ashley Cross is that bounded by Parr Street, Commercial Road, Springfield Road and Church Road - mainly private houses - with one or two properties at the beginning of Britannia Road and Salterns Road.

It has been suggested (not proven) that the crossroads were once called Parkstone Cross, and an 1886 map, which accompanied a report of the Commissioners on the Parish Boundaries, quoted the junction as 'Ashley Green'.

Victorian Times

The main growth in the area took place in Victorian times when Parkstone became a suburb for the wealthy and a haven from overcrowding and squalor from which the old town of Poole then suffered. The Dorsetshire and County Directory of 1851 mentions *'a healthy and pleasant site studded with pretty houses and mansions'*.

The slopes of Parkstone also began to attract visitors and the guide books of the time advertised its mild climate and salubrious surroundings as the *'Menton of England'*. The opening of the railway station (Parkstone-on-Sea) in 1874 further encouraged the growth of the area.

Trams started operating through Ashley Cross in 1901, and it then boasted a bustling shopping centre; when the tram lines were taken up in 1930, more traffic began to use Commercial Road/Bournemouth Road as a main route between Poole and Bournemouth. Shopping was a relaxed affair in those days - you gave your order to the shopkeeper, having first inspected the meat or fish, and it was delivered to your home later in the day; or in the case of a weekly order from the grocer, he would come to you to take your order!

In 1966 an 80 year old Britannia Road resident, Mrs Ethel A **Symonds**, was interviewed for the local paper. Her memories of Ashley Cross remind us that in her youth there were still plenty of open spaces around the area. There was nothing to interrupt the view from Britannia Road, which was lined with horse chestnut trees, to Poole Park and the immediate surroundings were of orchards with the blacksmith's forge just across the way in Salterns Road. Mrs **Symonds** remembered Mr **Farwell** and his donkey cart, who used to bring up from Poole Quay salted Newfoundland fish, and rabbits from surrounding estates at one shilling (5p) a time.

Other people remember the 1930's - the early morning paper train at Parkstone station with all the papers dumped on the platform, and the fishmongers waiting there for their boxes of fish; Granny **Pitman** selling sweets through the window of her cottage on the corner of Commercial/Curzon Road and doughnuts from a baker in Parr Street. One lad used to earn 6d (2^1/$_2$p) for weeding a drive in Ardmore Road and remembers the copse which belonged to 'Laurel Bank' in Station Road which eventually became Parkstone Motor Company and later Homelake House. Along that stretch there was a lady who bred *'sausage dogs'* - it is believed her name was Miss **Clinton**. *'Happy'* Prime, a shopkeeper, is remembered by many residents who grew up in the 1930's - he was called Happy because he was so miserable!

The Rolladrome (Rollerdrome) cropped up many times in conversation with older people. Its first site was Walters Garage/Derek **Warwick**, opposite Parkstone Post Office, and later in Church Road when it eventually became a dance hall - Ernie **Bull's** dance band is remembered and one lady recalls wearing a long dress to attend a Saturday night event. There was an archway leading to the Rolladrome from Commercial Road.

An old Scout of 1st Poole has not forgotten that in 1913 they marched from Poole to *'Parkstone Skating Rink'* to attend a Grand Rally where they enjoyed a great feast! In 1934 the building was converted into the First Church of Christ Scientist, and is now listed as a building of architectural merit.

Good Food

In the 1930's there were eight butchers in Ashley Cross and now, in 1995, there is only one - The Real Meat Company at 14 Bournemouth Road. Noel **Rigney** is the proprietor and he only sells additive free meat from a farm in Wiltshire where the livestock are traditionally reared. Coming to Ashley Cross in 1992, he took over the butcher's shop run for 30 years by Mr R G **Froud** until his retirement. Mr and Mrs **Froud** will be remembered by many people for they also ran the adjacent fish shop for 20 years. Mrs **Froud's** parents lived next door to Augustus **John** in Ringwood Road, and her father (H. **Curtis**, Haulier) was the first person to open an account with the Ashley Cross branch of Lloyds Bank.

Parkstone Fisheries, with greengrocery, is now run by Alan and Maureen **Lang**; and with Bennett's the bakers also there, that particular stretch of Bournemouth Road is now well worth a shopping expedition.

The old interior of the pharmacy in Station Road, with its wooden counters, glass carboys, medicine bottles and original hand written prescriptions is now on permanent display at the Waterfront Museum on Poole Quay. In 1918 Mr Percy **Cartledge** was the pharmacist, then Mr H C **Foster** who was there for many years, followed by Mr K **Sims** and now Mr **Ritchie**.

Evidence of another chemist's shop can still be seen further up Station Road on the corner with Approach Road. It is now Isabel's Restaurant and the name of J A **Haynes** is visible on the brass plate around the shop front, and other old items of interest are kept inside. The pharmacy was also an Off Licence - not so unusual in those days, as it might now be. Mr **Haynes** took his part in the civic life of Poole as a Councillor and was much involved with Scouting in the area. His brother, A B **Haynes** was also a pharmacist - in Broadstone it is believed.

Many people will also remember Mr Roger **Hand**, who died not long ago. His pharmacy was in Bournemouth Road on Post Office Parade - a Mr G H **Thomas** had been there in 1961 and Mr Albert George **Dunningham** in 1939. In the 1960's to 1970's Mr P F **Hand**, brother of Roger **Hand**, ran the ironmongers which was also on Post Office Parade.

Drs P **Forbes**, H **Whalen** and S **Lewis** occupy a purpose built surgery in a corner of the Commercial Road car park, fronting Wessex Road. This practice was once in Springfield Road and before that at Holmdale in Osborne Road by Parkstone Station. Dr Donald **Campbell** went into practice there in 1938, just before the beginning of the Second World War, and by the time he had returned from serving in the Forces, he had only a small nucleus of patients to look after; the National Health Service was not then in operation and Dr **Campbell** had to gradually build up his own practice. In due time Dr R M **Savage** took over, together with Dr K E **Marsh** and Dr K F **Strachan** in Poole. The site of Holmdale now holds a small block of flats.

Parkstone Park

Parkstone Park is sometimes referred to as *'The Green'*, although it may be noted in the 1890 map on the inside front cover that the space between Britannia and Salterns Roads is marked as *'Parkstone Green'*. Previous names have been Three Acre Field and Victoria Park - opened for public use in 1888, it commemorated Queen Victoria's Golden Jubilee the previous year.

The land was acquired from Lord **Wimborne** in exchange for other Corporation land and the valuation at the time was £400 per acre. The following description appeared in the 1918 Kelly's Directory:

'Parkstone Park is in the centre of Parkstone, a rising parish within the Borough, and comprises a little over three acres and was exchanged for other lands belonging to the Borough, and laid out at the public expense at a cost of £560. It contains some very fine trees and has a centre walk or promenade with a large terracotta fountain, the basin of which is stocked with gold and silver fish. Designed and carried out by Mr John **Elford**, *Borough Surveyor, who also designed Poole Park'.*

The Park was originally surrounded by an iron fence but this was removed in 1927 to give a more attractive lay-out. The official opening of Parkstone Park occurred in January 1890 when the **Prince of Wales**, later **King Edward VII**, came to Poole to open Poole Park.

In 1983, the 150th anniversary of St Peter's Church and School, a tradition was born with a midsummer fair being held in Parkstone Park (or on The Green!), and each succeeding year a similar event has taken place.

Memories of Ashley Cross would not be complete without mention of watchmaker Patrick **Beeney** in Parr Street. His father Bernard started the business there in 1932 and it is only in recent years that the shop has closed. In Commercial Road, Mr A E **Epps** the jeweller was at no 127 with 'Figgy' **Fudge** before him; and further along that same side 'The Bouquet' was run by Mr **Chidwick** for many years before Mr and Mrs **Luxford** and latterly Mr and Mrs John **Davies**, who ran it as Cherries the Delicatessen.

The Religious Community

ⓘ St Peter's Church

The Vicars

Reverend James Parr	1833-1853
Reverend Charles F Booker	1853-1858
Reverend John Parr MA	1858-1872
Reverend Ernest Edward Dugmore	1872-1910
Reverend the Hon R E Adderley MA	1910-1933
Reverend A J G Hawes PhD	1933-1937
Reverend Hugh Sherlock MA	1937-1946
Reverend H J Coulson B Litt AKC	1946-1970
Reverend C Kemp-Buck MA	1971-1974
Reverend P R Huxham MA	1974-1992
Reverend N Lloyd BTh STh	1992

■

The heart of Ashley Cross is St Peter's Church which stands on an island site surrounded by Parr Street, St Peter's Road and Church Road. The present church is the second building on the site. Before 1833 the Tithing of Parkstone formed part of the large parish of Great Canford and those residents wishing to worship had to travel up to five miles. In 1833 the Tithing of Parkstone was separated and became an independent Parish with a church of its own dedicated to St Peter and occupying the same site as the present building.

At that time the Parish included most of the present Parish of All Saints' Branksome Park, the whole of St Luke's and St Osmund's Parishes and the conventional districts of the Holy Angels at Salterns (Lilliput) and the Transfiguration at Canford Cliffs (Chaddesley Glen).

The Consecration

A lengthy legal Document dated 26th day of September 1833 headed *"Parkstone new Church and Church Yard - Sentence of Consecration"* states

'that more than six hundred persons resident in Parkstone a Tything in the said Parish of Great Canford and that three hundred at least of such persons resided upwards of 2 miles from any existing

church and within one mile of the Site whereon the New Church had been erected'.

The church was consecrated on Thursday 26th September 1833 by George Henry Lord Bishop of Bath and Wells, acting for Robert Lord Bishop of Bristol *'on account of illness being unable to attend in person'*, whose diocese included the county of Dorset. The Sentence of Consecration describes the site as *'that piece or parcel of land as the same as was then enclosed containing by admeasurement three roods and six perches to be the same (a little more or less) being therefore part of an ancient enclosure containing sixteen acres (more or less)'* and pronounced and appointed the said Church by the Name or Style of *"The Church of St Peter in the Tything of Parkstone in the Parish of Great Canford in the county of Dorset"*.

The original building (1833) was of rough stone plastered within and without and was of the style nicknamed *'Churchwardens Gothic'*; substantially built it had a pinnacled tower and when seen from a distance was not unpicturesque.

The second church building was described thus in Kelly's Directory of 1939 *'the church of St Peter, partly rebuilt in 1876 and again in 1892 and 1901, is built of Purbeck stone with Bath stone dressings in the Early English style consisting of a chancel with chapel and ambulatory, transepts and five bays of the nave. There are 1000 sittings, and the register dates from the year 1833'.*

Mention is made of St Lawrence's - a small church situated on Sandbanks Road - as being connected with St Peter's, and this was between the junction with Britannia Road and the railway bridge.

St Peter's Church and School, Parkstone 1833-1983

The Parr Connection

Parr Street, which runs alongside St Peter's, commemorates a family of lawyers who were closely involved with the church. Robert Henning **Parr**, Town Clerk to Poole, and his solicitor brother, John Edward **Parr** were the founders of St Peter's and two other members of the family were among the first incumbents - Reverend James **Parr** 1833-1853 and Reverend (later Canon) John **Parr** MA 1858-1872.

St Mary's Church at Longfleet also dates from 1833 with the building of both churches being completed at the same time - St Mary's was consecrated the day before St Peter's. The founder of St Mary's Church, The Hon W F S **Ponsonby** of Canford (later Lord de Mauley) had intended it to be a church for both Longfleet and Parkstone, but because some thought it too far from Ashley Cross and since Ponsonby was disliked by many as the patron of the Poole Liberals, St Peter's was built as a rival place of worship with the assistance of the Conservative Parr family.

Population Increase

In 1872 there were signs that the population of Parkstone was likely to increase considerably during the next few years. The town of Bournemouth, remembered by many people as only a fishing village, was becoming an important health resort whilst Poole, whose ancient trade with Newfoundland had almost ceased, was reviving by reason of the building enterprises in Bournemouth. The nearest railway stations then were Hamworthy to the west and Bournemouth Central to the east, but a railway line between Poole and Bournemouth was progressing, and Parkstone's own station opened in 1874.

It became evident that the church erected in 1833 had to be superseded by a larger building. Since Canon Parr had succeeded in freeing it from the evil of pew rents, there were no difficulties on that score, and the building itself was so unworthy of its purpose that no question of mere enlargement could be entertained. So it was that in 1875 the first steps were taken to replace the now inadequate and rapidly disintegrating old church.

The following is a report from the weekly *"Parkstone Reminder"* dated September 1875:

*'At a Meeting of the Church Society the chief business before the Meeting was the scheme for a new Church. The present was most unsatisfactory; it was much too small, it was hideously ugly, and was tumbling to pieces. The Vicar had caused plans for a really beautiful and substantial building to be prepared; a building which could be erected on its present site, over and enclosing the present miserable structure. It could be perfected by degrees, would provide the parish with a Church suitable to its needs, and, what was important of all, the proposed church would be somewhat more worthy of its great purpose - the worship of Almighty God. The Vicar proceeded to lay his proposal before the meeting. "He was willing at once to begin his part, viz: to build the Chancel in a style suitable to the dignity of the purpose to which it would be dedicated. He would trust the parishioners to accomplish their part by building the Transepts, Nave, and Tower, by degrees. We wanted a Church which should be able to meet the requirements of this increasing neighbourhood, and he thought it would be only right to leave part of the work to be done in the next generation. Did the meeting believe that the parishioners would come forward and help?...Eventually the two following resolutions were proposed by Sir William Brown, seconded by Mr H R **Dugmore**, and carried: 1. That it is not expedient that the Vicar begin to build his part, viz: the Chancel, until a subscription list has been formed for the parishioners' part, viz: the Naves Transepts and Tower, or part thereof. 2. That a subscription list be shortly opened to enable the parishioners, and others to shew what they are willing to undertake in this matter'.*

The first subscription list, £1497.15s.8d. was published in January 1876. The foundation stone of the new edifice, later to be described as the *'Cathedral of Poole'* was laid on August 1st 1876

'amidst the pleasantest surroundings of beautiful weather, and a large concourse of sympathetic friends. Early in the day the old flag-staff was re-erected on the Church tower, and a red cross was hoisted. About 3.30 a procession formed at St Peter's Schoolrooms, and began to march upward to the place fixed for the ceremony. First came the St Peter's Schools with their new and effective banners; the banner of the Guild of the Good Shepherd being conspicuous; then, preceded by the processional Cross, came the Choir and Clergy, the Vicar bringing up the rear with the Reverend L Dawson-Damer, the Rural Dean.'

Lady Cornelia **Guest**, accompanied by her husband Sir Ivor **Guest**, laid the foundation stone with a silver-plated trowel handed to her by the architect, Mr Frederick **Rogers** of London. Inserted beneath the stone was a glass stoppered bottle containing a parchment with the relevant historical information; and it is recorded that a collection taken at the service, together with offerings from the 8.00am Celebration amounted to £75.17s.6d.

The consecration of the first part of the new church consisting of the present lofty and spacious Chancel with its Ambulatories, together with two Transepts and the central space, now forming the two eastern bays of the Nave took place on 18th December 1878. The day was a beautiful one, in the midst of very stormy weather, and work had continued all through the previous night so that the new building would be ready for the opening service at 7.00am. The western end of the old nave was left standing for the accommodation of the congregation for the time being.

There was a fresh architect, Mr John L **Pearson** MA, for the next stage of the church, and on Tuesday 14th June 1881 the corner stone of the Vestries and Organ Chamber was laid with the ceremony taking place after the 5.00pm Evensong. Another glass bottle, containing an inscription recording the fact and date of the occasion, was buried for posterity; and this time the collection amounted to £52.14.7^1/$_2$d.

By December 1881 the Vestries and Organ Chamber were complete and work then began on the three bays of the Nave and Aisles; and The Bishop, Dr **Wordsworth**, performed the Dedication ceremony on 1st July 1892.

Completion

The new St Peter's church was now nearing completion, and on the 7th July 1900 the ceremony of the laying of the south-western Cornerstone of the Nave took place. In attendance were the children of St Peter's and Salterns Sunday Schools; and the Vicar and the Archdeacon met the Mayor, Sheriff and Councillors and conducted them to their places in the nave.

A special Office was commenced by the Vicar, with responses sung by the Choir. This special Office, with modifications, was used at the Stone-laying at Truro Cathedral in 1880 and was authorised by the Bishop for this occasion at St Peter's.

Yet another glass bottle was deposited in a cavity underneath the stone containing a copy of the *'Parkstone Reminder'* and relevant information on a parchment:

"The south-west corner-stone of the second Church of St. Peter, Parkstone, was layed by Edith, widow of Reverend Lionel Dawson Damer, Canon of Salisbury, on the Festival of S.Peter the Apostle, in the 1,900th year of our Redemption, the Right Reverend John Wordsworth being Bishop of Salisbury; the Ven. Francis Briggs Sowter Archdeacon of Dorset; the Rev. William Okes Parish Rural Dean of the Poole portion of the Whitchurch Deanery; Ernest Edward Dugmore Vicar of Parkstone; in the 63rd year of the glorious reign of our gracious Sovereign Lady Victoria, Queen and Empress, the Right Worshipful J A Cocker being Mayor

of the Borough of Poole, and Alexander Kelly and Edward Ferraby, Churchwardens, of Parkstone.'

The architect's handwritten Specification of Works for the completion of St Peter's Church, dated January 1900, set out the type and quality of stone to be selected, the amount of timber required and the number of hours needed from the various workmen - excavator, scaffolder, waller, stone mason, horse and cart man, labourer, tiler, carpenter and joiner, smith and founder, plumber, glazier and painter. Instructions for the mason regarding the stone were quite specific *'the Bath stone to be from the Corsham Down Quarries and carefully selected of the best description and quality. The Portland Stone to be from the Whitbed of the best approved quarries. The Purbeck Stone to be of the best and hardest description. The whole of the Stone to be approved by the Architect and to be free from sand holes, vents, and all other defects and to be worked to lie on its natural bed and set'.*

By 25th September 1901, the second St Peter's Church was complete, with the exception of the spire which had been planned on the North side; to this day the church still lacks that spire.

1901 was the 68th anniversary of the original foundation of the church and on Wednesday evening, 25th September the completion of the second St Peter's Church was celebrated.

*'The Service began with a penitential preparation, consisting of the Miserere followed by the Veni Creator and prayers. Then the Clergy and Choir proceeded to the west end of the Nave and awaited the Bishop, who announced his arrival by the customary triple knock made with his pastoral staff on the new south door, and by the Versicle, "Open me the gates of righteousness, that I may go into them and give thanks unto the Lord". This was duly followed by a response from those inside, and the Churchwardens opened the door, admitting the Bishop, who was accompanied by his domestic Chaplain (Rev. W. A. **Crokat**) and the Rev. C. M. **Gane**. The Bishop passed through the double line of the Churchwardens and Sidesmen, and taking his place among the Clergy below the west wall, proceeded with the form of re-opening and blessing the Church. The Bishop, Clergy, and Choir then moved up the Church to the Chancel, singing the Psalm "Latatus sum". Then the Te Deum was sung to a Gregorian tone, the Bishop, with certain of the Clergy, standing before the Altar, and after dedicatory and benedictory prayers, his lordship preached on the nature of Church Worship. The beautiful Dedication Hymn, "O Thou, Who sitt'st enthroned above", was then sung, and a collection for the Church completion Fund was made. Prayers and a Blessing concluded the Service.'*

Inside the Church

Canon Earnest Edward **Dugmore** played a prominent part in the early life of St Peter's; he was Vicar for 38 years from 1872-1910 and was described as *'a saintly character who inspired his parishioners'* and was remembered with love and awe by those who came into contact with him. The second church was built under his patronage and inspiration, and it was from his notes that a history of the church 1872-1910 was written. He was probably the instigator of the weekly paper *The Parkstone Reminder'* (copies in Poole Reference Library) which ran from a date just previous to 1880, until 1912. *The Parkstone Reminder'* was printed by the *'Vicar's Private Printing Office, Parkstone'* and published by *'J J Miller, Cyprus House, Parkstone'*.

The Chapel of the Holy Name, with the beautiful Reredos, was built by Canon **Dugmore** as a memorial to his family. Designed on the lines of the great screen in Winchester Cathedral, the Reredos is made of Australian timber with a set of figures carved by the famous sculptor, Herr Zwincke of Oberammergau. The figures represent Our Lord on the Cross with the Blessed Virgin and St John on either side and six statuettes - SS Ignatius, Cyprian, Athanasius, Bede, Bernard and Anselm.

The High Altar in The Sanctuary contains another set of figures by Herr Zwincke, with those at the front representing the twelve Apostles. Also within The Sanctuary on the north side is the canopied carved oak Bishop's Throne with the Arms of the See; the wrought iron Chancel Screen which was designed by the second architect of St Peter's, Mr J L Pearson, and the beautiful Sanctuary lamps were given in 1877 by Mr Cavendish **Bentinck**, godson of King George IV and owner, at that time, of Brownsea Island.

Canon **Dugmore** is himself commemorated in a stained glass window in the South Chancel, together with one in memory of his successor, Reverend The Honourable R E **Adderley** MA (1910-1933). This latter window incorporates two Archangels over panels containing representations of St Cecilia playing the organ and David playing the harp, symbolizing Praise.

'Gloria in Excelsis' is the subject of the central light of the East window given by Reverend John **Parr** MA, Vicar 1858-1872, in memory of his father, John Edward **Parr**, and portrays the symbols seen by St John in the Apocalyptic vision.

Dating from 1909, the pulpit is made of Bath stone with cornice and column of Purbeck marble, and the richly-carved canopy is of oak. The design is exceptionally beautiful and the carvings on the front represent the Ordination and Mission of the Apostles flanked by statuettes of St Gregory the Great and St Augustine.

The font at the West end of the Nave is constructed of alabaster and marble; the elaborately carved oak canopy was added as a thank offering from a parishioner.

The rich foliage carving of the Capitals in the main arcade is in tune with the Early English character of the building, and of particular interest is the respond at the West end of the North arcade. This was carried out at the cost of a former Bishop of Salisbury in order to commemorate the nearly 25 years in which he had ministered to the Church. To mark this as the Bishop's gift, a small figure was introduced into the conventional foliage. The figure represents St Osmund, the first Bishop of Old Sarum and he is holding a crozier in one hand and a model of the Cathedral in the other.

St Peter's has eight tubular bells given in 1887; and the Processional Cross, given in 1895 as a thank offering, is finely worked in silver on an ebony pole.

Erected in 1933 to mark the centenary of the building of the first St Peter's, the South Porch has a frieze of carved heads of Saints.

The Scouting Link

Poole is the birthplace of the Boy Scouts for it was on Brownsea Island in 1907 that **Baden-Powell** held his experimental camp. The youth organisation which he founded went on to become worldwide and formed the basis for Scouts and Guides of all ages, with both organisations still flourishing today.

A marriage, a christening and the Team Ministry closely link St Peter's Church with **Baden-Powell** and with Scouting. St Mary's Church on Brownsea is part of the St Peter's Team Ministry (together with St Osmund), and the clergy make regular trips across the Harbour to conduct services, particularly in the summer months when Scouts and Guides are camping on the island.

In 1912, on Wednesday 30th October, Reverend the Honourable R E **Adderley** conducted the marriage of Olave St Clair **Soames** to Lieutenant-General Sir Robert Stephenson Smyth **Baden-Powell**, KCB (later Lord **Baden-Powell** of Gilwell) at St Peter's Church. It was a simple ceremony attended only by close family and friends, and Olave **Soames**, who then lived at Grey Rigg in Lilliput, had just one bridesmaid - B-P's sister Agnes, who together with her brother was the Founder of the Girl Guides.

The event was in complete contrast to that envisaged by the journalists of the day, who indicated that the date for the wedding would be 1st December, that it would be held in the Lilliput parish church with a large congregation, that a Boy Scout Guard of Honour would line the route from Grey Rigg to the church and that they would be inspected by their Founder after the service. The reasoning behind this speculation was that **Baden-Powell** was famous not only as the Founder of the Boy Scouts but was a national hero as Defender of Mafeking 1899-1900 during the Boer War. Further interest would have been created by the fact that **Baden-Powell** was 30 years older than his bride - he was 53 and Olave just 23 years of age.

The marriage was indeed a happy one, and of their three children the eldest, Peter, was christened at St Peter's. A Memorial Service for Lord **Baden-Powell** was held at the church in 1941; a Thanksgiving Service for Lady **Baden-Powell** in 1977 - she was the first woman Freeman of Poole (in May 1950) and had been World Chief Guide for many years.

Parish Magazine 1913

Although the weekly '*Parkstone Reminder*' was no longer produced after 1912, the monthly '*St Peter's, Parkstone Parish Magazine*' flourished, and in 1944 had as its title '*Outlook' Parish Magazine of the Lower Parkstone Team - St Peter's, St Osmund's, St Mary's.*

The Parish Magazine for September 1913, (price 1d) was printed by Ralph and Brown, Archway Works, Parkstone. The Vicar was Reverend The Honourable R E **Adderley**, editor was Reverend A R **Fernsby** of 'Seafield', Church Crescent and the Churchwardens were Messrs G C A **Kentish** and A R **Solly**. Of the seventeen sidesmen, one was H A Prime, who had a small advertisement in the magazine extolling the virtues of '*Good Teas and Home Cooked Hams*' in his grocer's shop. The Organist and Choirmaster was Mr C E **Rabbetts** of Mentone Road and the Verger and Sacristan was Mr J M **Roberts** of St Peter's Road.

Listings of services included The Chapel of the Holy Angels at Salterns and The Chapel of the Transfiguration at Canford Cliffs; and advance notice given of the Dedication Festival on 26th September to commemorate the 80th anniversary of the Consecration of the church.

The '*Parochial Notes*' mentioned a concert in aid of the '*Missions to Seamen*' to be held in the Parkstone Skating Rink, and under the heading of the Diocesan Inspector's Report on St Peter's Day School, there is a long list of examination results.

Societies and charities were numerous and diverse ranging from the Community of St. Michael and All Angels, Bloemfontein, S Africa through the Parkstone Missions Union to the Guild of the Good Shepherd and the Diocesan Society for Preventive and Rescue Work. The District Nurse had a heading all to herself, she was Nurse **Bagshaw** of 'Winnington' in North Road.

Almost half of the magazine was taken up with advertising. A London company were promoting their 1914 Gospel Stamps, available either in two different kinds of Album or in packets of 25 at the usual rate of one penny. Overseas customers were advised to order *at once*.

Among the local advertisements were J A Haynes 'The Mentone Pharmacy', J A Hawkes suggesting that 'your Boots are more conspicuous than anything else you wear', Ingram Nurseries, grocers Leverett and Frye, J S Coles Colliery Agent, F Bugler promoting 'Fish! Fish! Eat Fish and more of it', Bonnett's Stores, Geo W Lush - Coal, Corn, Flour, Hay, Seed and Forage Merchant and H G Dunford hiring out an Invalid's Pony Bath Chair at 1/6d per hour.

Parishioners

The life of any church is dependent on the support and dedication of its parishioners. Since 1833 there have obviously been a great number of lay people who have devoted themselves to St Peter's, but it is only possible to mention one or two by name.

In the July 1985 issue of '*Dorset Life*', Eric **George** wrote about Upper and Lower Parkstone and one of his personal memories was of Herbert Arthur **Ellis**. Known to all as "*Bertie*", he served as Sacristan and Verger under six different Vicars for over 50 years. He received the Royal Maundy from The Queen in Salisbury Cathedral in April 1974 and died later that year at the age of 80.

A log book written by Mr **Ellis** in his capacity as Verger tells us that in August 1959 he accompanied the Diocesan Architect to inspect the roof timbers and vaulting - '*found some woodworm damage etc*'; and in 1960 '*Boons of Poole Locksmiths picked lock and drilled off door of lower safe in Sacristy through breaking of spring in lock. Replaced with new lock and 3 keys*'. Mr John **Christie**, grandson of Mrs **Bonham-Christie**, in May 1961, invited The Vicar Reverend H J **Coulson**, the Churchwarden Mr P **Smith** and Mr **Ellis**, the Verger to inspect the fabric of St Mary's on Brownsea Island and to make future plans for the use of the church; it was decided that the Registers of Marriages, Baptisms and Burials would be brought back to St Peter's for safe keeping since St Mary's was very damp.

Later that year a new oil heating system was installed in St Peter's and several purchases made - new blue carpet for Blue Altar £20.0.0., Cross Bros filled in arch over Tower Screen to keep out draughts £20.0.0. and SEB cleaned all electrical fittings £18.0.0. A 12' radiator was installed in the South Transept at a cost of £88.0.0. in February 1962; and in April '*outside trunking from engine room to Sacristy to convey wind to Organ Chamber, was found necessary to have layer of Concrete to stop escape of wind to the Reservoir of Organ Chamber*'. Never a dull moment, it seems.

The name of Freddie **Buncehall** will remind many folk of their younger days for he was connected with the youth of St Peter's for 50 years in his capacity as Group Scout Leader, and was affectionately known as *'Skip'*. For a few years, he also held the post of Verger. His funeral in January 1981 was described as the local equivalent of a State funeral with over 500 people at the church.

George **Appleby-Smith** was another man who devoted himself to the young people at St Peter's. Among the congregation at his Memorial Service on 8th July 1983 were many who were Wolf Cubs and Boy Scouts under his leadership of the 6th Parkstone Troop, including Reverend Stephen **Lake**, Vicar of St Aldhelm's, who gave the address.

Father Peter

Father Peter
Courtesy: Reverend
Diana Newman

In 1974 Reverend Peter R **Huxham** MA, was appointed Vicar of the United Benefice of Parkstone St Peter with Branksea and Parkstone St Osmund. A locally born man, Father Peter was made a Canon of Salisbury Cathedral in 1985, and was at St Peter's for 18 years until taking up his present post, in 1992, as Chaplain at Taunton Hospital in Somerset.

A familiar figure around and about Ashley Cross, Father Peter was popular, not only with his parishioners but with civic dignitaries and fellow clergy of all denominations.

Many tributes and anecdotes about him appeared in the parish magazine before he and his wife Jane departed for Somerset, which gave an insight into Father Peter's versatile character, his sense of humour and devotion to duty.

His tangible accomplishments included the parish centre, overhaul of St Peter's organ and procurement of a modern rectory; he fought to retain the old St Peter's School in Parr Street, but nevertheless gave his indefatigable support to the new Baden-Powell and St Peter's School in Mill Lane, as borne out by the following extract from the parish magazine of June 1989:

'Where Are They All Going? people asked as they saw 400 pupils from Baden-Powell and St Peter's School walking in a happy but orderly crocodile across the crossing at Ashley Cross. They were like a happy flock of starlings and a great deal more colourful in their cheerful red pullovers and gold and red ties, and they certainly sang better than the birds, when they raised the roof with their Ascension Day hymns at the school service in St Peter's. It was good to have the children, teachers, governors, parents, grandparents and parishioners all worshipping together, and nearly 50 received Holy Communion. It was a joyful symbol of the unity which has been so quickly formed from our two former schools, and a great credit to all the staff and pupils.'

Under Father Peter's direction, seven men held their first curacies in the parishes and were grateful for his positive and relevant training coupled with shared ideas, informal learning and a great deal of fun and fellowship.

In 1971 Father Peter became the first Mayor's Chaplain who was not Rector of St James in Poole, and his popularity was such that several successive mayors also appointed him as their Chaplain.

Tributes in the parish magazine described him as a *'wise counsellor of deep understanding and perception'*; and Percy **Tilley**, churchwarden at the time, wrote *'the fellowship to be found at St Peter's is a demonstration of Father Peter's outstanding Christian leadership and pastoral care'*.

The Reverend Mrs Diana J **Newman**, now Senior Curate, spoke of her long association with Father Peter - *'he has a wonderful sense of humour and a great love of people, a tremendous dedication to his duties and a meticulous approach to all his liturgy. He was a great organiser and remains a superb priest'.*

First Woman Deacon

Diana **Newman** was the first Deacon in the parish to be trained by Father Peter, and was made Deacon in 1986 when the Church of England first admitted women to the Ordained Ministry.

On Saturday, 11th June 1994 Diana **Newman** was ordained, with 37 other women, in Salisbury Cathedral by the Bishop of Salisbury, The Right Reverend Dr David **Stancliffe**; and the next day Canon Peter **Huxham** attended her first celebration of the Eucharist at St Peter's. This was an historic event, not only because of the Church's new rules but, St Peter's as a High Church parish might not have accepted a woman priest at all without Father Peter's influence.

Father Nigel

In the second half of 1992, Reverend Nigel **Lloyd** was welcomed as Team Rector of the Benefice of Parkstone St Peter with St Osmund and St Mary, Brownsea Island. Father Nigel, and his wife Jane and their two daughters, did not have far to come as he had, for eight years, been Rector at Lytchett Matravers and his previous post was as a curate at Sherborne Abbey.

Educated at Chaffyn Grove School in Salisbury and at Lancing College, Father Nigel spent many holidays sailing in Poole Harbour with his parents, who are both priests. Before preparing for the ministry he gained experience in the commercial world when working, for seven years, within the wine trade in London. Whilst at Lincoln Theological College, Father Nigel took a Degree in Theology from Nottingham University; and was later awarded an S Th Degree from the Archbishop of Canterbury for his work of *The Doctrine of Marriage in the Church of England'*. Ordained as a Deacon in Salisbury Cathedral in 1981, he then began his association with Dorset at Sherborne Abbey.

Having always had a deep interest in ecumenism, Father Nigel, whilst at Lytchett Matravers, began a Local Ecumenical Project in the village in partnership with the Methodist Church; and is now Secretary of the Salisbury Diocesan Ecumenical team as well as being the Anglican Ecumenical Officer for the Sherborne Episcopal area.

As the elected chairman of Baden-Powell St Peter's School in Mill Lane, Father Nigel is particularly keen to continue and strengthen the link between the church and the school, as well as supporting the vigorous youth organisations within St Peter's.

Reverend Jane Lloyd

On 11th June 1994 Jane **Lloyd**, together with Diana **Newman** and 36 other women, was ordained in Salisbury Cathedral. Like her husband, Jane worked in the commercial world before training in Theology; she is a Chartered Chemist, a Graduate of the Royal Institute of Chemistry and held a post with Burton Biscuits as the company chemist before taking a Postgraduate Diploma in Theology.

Jane worked full time for a year in the parish of St Nicholas, Lincoln before coming to Dorset, and in Sherborne moved to non-stipendiary ministry as their two daughters were born. It was whilst they were in Lytchett

St Peter's Church 12th June 1994
from left: Reverend Richard Davey, Reverend Jane Lloyd, Reverend Nigel Lloyd, Reverend Diana Newman, Reverend Alan Jeans, Mrs Jane Huxham, Reverend Peter Huxham.
Courtesy: Reverend Diana Newman

Matravers that the part-time chaplaincy at Poole Hospital became vacant, and Jane took that post, which soon developed into full time work. She now has an assistant and is responsible for leading a large chaplaincy team of part-time chaplains and volunteers at the hospital. As well as preaching and helping at St Peter's on an occasional basis, Jane regularly lectures at Bournemouth University and is in great demand as a speaker, particularly on matters of pastoral ministry.

Midsummer Fairs

In 1983 St Peter's church revived a tradition of holding fairs in Parkstone Park (on the Green). It was then the 150th anniversary of both the church and the school in Parr Street and the Regency Fayre on 18th June was opened by Lady **Butler**, widow of R A **Butler**, Conservative politician who had held numerous Government posts, including that of Minister for Education.

A similar event has taken place in mid-June each year, generally blessed with fine weather. A different theme is chosen each year, with money raised going towards specific projects, church funds and charities. The theme in 1985 was the 1940's when stallholders dressed in the appropriate fashions and £1700 was raised for church funds.

Harvest of Talents

At the end of September 1995 St Peter's held a week long *'Harvest of Talents'*. An event of this kind had not previously been organised by the church, and whilst part of the aim was fund raising, the main theme was that of *'outreach'* - an endeavour to *'gather in'* and involve members of the community who were unaware of the diverse church activities.

On the first Sunday, the Poole Sea Cadets Band headed a procession to the church from Parkstone Park, so setting the scene for the rest of the week.

Art demonstrations, music recitals and childrens workshops took place inside the church - a local potter demonstrated his work, the church was decorated with flowers and vestments and refreshments were available all through the day. Paintings by the local art group PEDAS (Poole and East Dorset Arts Society) were on display, as well as some from the Art and Spirituality Group run by Reverend Richard **Davey**.

The parish accounts had shown a shortfall of £6,000 for the year's running costs and it had been anticipated that only part of that sum would have been raised. However, the gift day at the end of the week was so successful tht the amount raised was just over the £6,000 needed.

The 'Harvest of Talents' week ended with a packed Harvest Festival on Sunday 1st October, when Thanks were given, not only for produce, vegetables and fruit, but for the hobbies and talents of individual people.

*Historical information for this chapter was taken from 'Records of the Church of St Peter, Parkstone: It's Re-Building and Memorials 1872 to 1910.' Author not specified, but most likely to have been Canon **Dugmore**.*

St Peter's Church - St George's Day Parade - 23rd April 1995 - Borough of Poole Scout Council, Poole East District.
From left: Reverend Richard Davey Curate, Mr John Ward Poole MP and his wife, Reverend Stephen Lake Borough Scout Chaplain.

ⅱ *Parkstone United Reformed Church*

(previously Congregational Church)

In June 1993 Parkstone United Reformed Church in Commercial Road celebrated the Centenary of the present building. The Minister, Reverend David **Bending**, conducted Services of Thanksgiving and a celebratory lunch was hosted by a former Minister (1942-1971) Reverend Walter **Dickinson**. Previously the Parkstone Congregational Church, the United Reformed Church was founded in 1972 through the union of the Congregational Church of England and Wales and the Presbyterian Church of England, with the Churches of Christ joining in 1981.

The first indication of nonconformist worship in the area comes from the list of licences to hold nonconformist services granted by the Quarter Sessions in the county of Dorset - *'Dwelling House of Thomas Knight, Parkstone, Presbyts, 4th October 1737'*. The Congregational connection in Parkstone, then *'an obscure and scattered hamlet'* was introduced in 1804 through the Skinner Street Congregational Church in Poole. The book *'Story of the Congregational Churches in Dorset'* by W **Densham** and J

Ogle published in 1899 mentions a Statement dated February 1st 1839, drawn up and signed by Reverend T **Durant**, indicating that 35 years earlier (1804) several Christian friends - Messrs J **Wadham**, J B **Brown**, T **Coward**, T **Butler**, D **Bird** and J **Spurrier** - started a Sunday School in a cottage rented from a Mr **Guy** to teach *'the heathen of Parkstone'*.

It appears that this initiative was successful and others continued their work with a Sunday evening and a week night service being conducted by Reverend **Durant**. At one time the Sunday School numbered as many as 90 scholars and subsequently a more suitable building was hired from a Mr W **Green**.

Reverend T **Durant** was untiring in his efforts to extend the gospel in the districts around Poole and it soon became necessary to find a more spacious property. Financial help came from a Poole resident Mrs **Bunn**, aunt of Mrs Martin **Kemp-Welch**, to *'rear a House of God in Parkstone'*; George **Gollop** was both architect and builder, Mr David **Tuck** took the contract for the masonry and the new place of worship opened on 6th March 1839. The total cost, including the land, was £1000 which was defrayed by Mrs **Bunn**, whose maiden name was **Buckland** and the new building in Chapel Lane was called *'Buckland Chapel'* to commemorate her generosity.

In 1863 it became possible, with financial assistance from Skinner Street Congregational Church, to appoint an Assistant Minister who divided his time between the two churches. The first man to hold this post was John **Fernie** - he only stayed 18 months before taking over a church in Durban for the Colonial Missionary Society, and was followed by John **Lockwood** BA, John George **Tolley** and D H **Richard**.

Independence

The need for pecuniary aid from the Skinner Street church gradually diminished and in 1885 it was felt that the time had come for Parkstone Church to enter upon an independent existence. The Charity Commissioners gave their consent to a separation and a new Trust Deed was prepared by them dated 6th October 1885. The new church was formed, with 57 members, on 12th November 1885 under the presidency of Reverend E **Evans**, pastor of the church in Poole, with Reverend W **Jackson** of Bournemouth assisting; the following being chosen to fulfil the office of deacon - John Sydney **Hudson**, Alfred Augustus **Allen**, Titus **Buckley**, Henry Hodges **Hayman**, Frederick **Piper** and John **Trumble**.

The first Pastor, William Plaskett **Dothie** MA, commenced his duties at Parkstone Congregational Church on 4th July 1886, and as membership increased the need for additional accommodation became apparent. It was decided to build a new church, relinquishing their old site, and half an acre of land in a central position on the main road was purchased from Lord **Wimborne** for £125. George **Lawson** was the architect and the work undertaken by Mr W H C **Curtis** of Poole for the sum of £3050.

Strenuous efforts in fund raising were made by the Pastor and church members and T J **Hankinson** Esq of Bournemouth laid the memorial stone on 10th November 1892; and a large meeting was held in the evening with James **Jackson** Esq of *'Danecourt'* in the chair. The opening ceremony of the new building on 22nd June 1893 was to have had Dr Newman **Hall** as the preacher but due to an accident he was unable to attend and his place was taken by Reverend A Seys **Howell** of Southampton with Sir George **Williams**, founder of the YMCA, presiding over the evening meeting. In their book *'Story of the Congregational Churches in Dorset'* Densham and Ogle describe the new church as *'attractive, substantial and capacious, worthy of fashionable Parkstone and a credit to the denomination'*.

Other people associated with both Skinner Street and Parkstone Congregational Church during the century 1800-1900 included Mr **Gollop** (father of George), Mr W B **Coward**, Martin **Kemp-Welch** Esq, Reverend and Mrs Walter **Gill**, John Sidney **Hudson** Esq JP, Reverend and Mrs James **Sewell** and Alfred A **Allen** Clerk of the Poole Justices of Peace. In the late 1890's Messrs Titus **Buckley**, J **Lindsay**, H H **Hayman**, A J **Strudwicke** and J **Finlayson** were deacons of the Parkstone church.

Pastoral Care

Between 1893 and 1917 the church flourished under the pastoral care of Reverend James William **Coulton** (1893-1903), and Reverend Willoughby **Gee** (1903-1917); and until 1941 under Reverend Herbert **Heywood** and Reverend George **McLuckie** BA. Youth work became a feature of the life of the church prior to the start of the Second World War, uniformed organisations were established, the organ rebuilt and the Youth Hut and Manse purchased.

The Congregation Magazine dated December 1940 included a letter from The Battalion The Green Howards from *'somewhere in England'* thanking the church members for the welcome the men received during their stay in Parkstone and mentioning the enjoyable and happy hours the Green Howards had spent at *'the club'*. During the war Forces Clubs all over the country were manned by volunteers so that Servicemen, wherever they were stationed, had somewhere to go in their off duty hours.

In the January 1941 issue the Minister Reverend G **McLuckie** wrote:-

'I want to thank all our ladies who have given themselves with such devotion throughout the year to the service of the troops in our own Canteen, and in the Canteen at Poole, which is run jointly by all the Churches - Established and Free. I can assure them, from the many testimonies that have reached me, that their service has been greatly appreciated by the men'.

Elsewhere in the magazine congratulations were given to Mr F S **Marshall** who had been appointed President of the Poole Association of the National Union of Teachers; and to two young people on their musical successes - Margaret **Gantzer** Royal Academy of Music, Piano Grade 7, with Distinction and Joyce **Kinsbury** Royal Acadamy of Music, Piano Grade 5, with Distinction.

The social activities concerning the Young People's club were reported. On 21st December 1941 Mr and Mrs **Bennett** gave a fish and chip party to the Club in celebration of their son Ronald's 21st birthday. Everyone spent a most enjoyable evening and Ron was presented with a pair of silver cufflinks and also congratulated on his engagement to Doreen **Allen**. At the same time a silver jam spoon was given to Mr and Mrs **Bennett** who were celebrating their 25th wedding anniversary.

The other social event, a New Year's Eve party held in the Club Hut, *'was attended by a large number of club members and members of HM Forces who enjoyed the dancing, games and delicious refreshments'*. The MC was Mr **Shilton** and he and his wife were presented with an electric bedside lamp and a bouquet of chrysanthemums as a token of appreciation for all they did for the Young Peoples' Club.

The marriage on 25th December of Joseph Frank **Wellman** and Kate Victoria **Orchard** was recorded in the magazine, as was the Baptism on 15th December of Arthur

Parkstone United Reformed Church

Harold **Batterson**, son of Mr and Mrs H E **Batterson** - Harold **Batterson** and his wife gave many years of service to the Cubs and Scouts (5th Parkstone red/yellow scarves) at the Church.

Reverend Walter Dickinson

A great number of people will remember, and be grateful for, the Ministry of Reverend Walter **Dickinson** who was Pastor for 29 years from 1942-1971. During his time the church played a leading role, not only in the Parkstone area, but through his efforts encompassed the whole of Poole. He recalls that he had the privilege of preaching in each church in Poole, of whatever denomination, over the 25 years.

Born a Yorkshireman but brought up in Lancashire, Reverend Walter **Dickinson** trained at Nottingham Theological College and Nottingham University, and was Inspector of Schools for the Free Churches of Nottinghamshire before coming to Ashley Cross.

His arrival coincided with the difficult and uncertain middle years of the Second World War, and his pastoral work as Chaplain to the Royal Marines at Hamworthy meant that he was a constant visitor to the Base. A problem arose with the postponement of D-Day in June 1944 by 24 hours. For obvious security reasons no-one was allowed out and Reverend Walter **Dickinson**, who was visiting the Base to be with the men before they went across the Channel, was at first refused permission to leave. Only after explaining that he had other pressing pastoral duties to conduct, was he permitted to depart!

Reverend Walter **Dickinson** gave freely of his time and energy and many organisations benefited from his presence on their committees. He was the Mayor's Chaplain in 1963, served on Poole Education Committee for 25 years and was Governor of both Parkstone and Poole grammar schools.

As District Secretary of Dorset Congregational Churches, which later became United Reformed Churches, Dorset District, he helped arrange the *'Religion and Life Week'* which packed the Bournemouth Pavilion every day, the highlight of which was the visit of the Archbishop of Canterbury, Dr William **Temple**. He instigated the opening of Oxfam in Poole, started the Womens World Day of Prayer, and his was the first church in Poole to set up a luncheon club in the late 1940's which was eventually handed over to the then WVS, now WRVS.

Youth Organisations

Parkstone Congregational Church was a thriving community with very active youth organisations - Scouts and Cubs were run by Harold **Batterson** and his wife for many years. Their daughter, Vivienne ran the Brownies;

Young People's Club Band 1938
Violins - Eric Austin & - Hardy, Drummer - Alec Shelton, Compere - Jack Squires, Accordians - Eric Bennett, Edgar Elton and Ron Bennett, Vocalist - John Travers, Piano - Mrs Austin, Banjo - Nancy Tompkins, Clarinet - Bernard Dyer.
Courtesy: Alex Wilson

Mrs Alice **Suckling** from Bird's Hill Road, was Captain of the 7th Parkstone Girl Guide Company with Barbara **Dutfield** (née **Pollard**) as her Lieutenant. Barbara eventually went to the 1st Parkstone Guide Company which had their headquarters in the Langdon Road Guide Hall, which opened in 1931. The Youth Fellowship met three times a week and at various times had flourishing drama and music groups.

Memorial Window

A Memorial Window and a new Pulpit were dedicated at a special service conducted by Reverend Walter **Dickinson** on Sunday 26th February 1950. *Those of the Fellowship Who Gave Their Lives in the two Wars 1914-1918 and 1939-45'* and the congregation remembered, with proud thanksgiving:

> 1914-1918 E Allen, M Allen, T A Dix, A J Gritten,
> H F Hayman, J W Hayman, H S Hayward,
> J W Hayward, C H W Homer, E H McKay, S Sargent,
> W Temple, C J Withers.

> 1939-1945 V H Cattle, R M T Draper, N C Reinelt.

The Memorial Window was the personal gift of Mrs H E **Norton** in memory of her husband Ernest J **Norton**, who was a deacon of the church. Artist Hugh **Easton**, who was responsible for the Battle of Britain Window in Westminster Abbey was the designer, and the window depicts Jesus preaching by the shore of the Sea of Galilee.

The Tower

A steeple once adorned the tower of Parkstone Congregational Church, as can be seen in early photographs; but it became unsafe and was too costly to repair and in the early 1980's was removed.

The tower itself is of particular interest to church architects for the vents originally had the specific purpose of acting as regulating shutters for the central heating system. The vents controlled the inflow of air from the tower so that hot air was circulated throughout the building. It was quite a complicated matter, and Reverend **Dickinson** recalls that many years ago only one deacon knew how to operate the shutters satisfactorily. Mr **Best** apparently said, *'I am not telling anyone how it all works and the secret will die with me'*; and this is exactly what happened. The next person in charge of the central heating had a tricky problem to solve!

Media Fame

Reverend Walter **Dickinson** became familiar with conducting services for both radio and television. On 29th August 1954 the Morning Service on the West of England BBC Home Service was broadcast from Parkstone Congregational Church reaching an estimated 180,000 people, and a service in the 1960's was televised. He also conducted a Songs of Praise from St Peter's Church, Ashley Cross on radio, and one for television from St James Church in Poole.

The 70th anniversary celebrations in 1963 at Parkstone Congregational Church coincided with the 21st year of the pastorate of Reverend Walter **Dickinson** and many tributes were paid to him on that occasion.

At a social gathering, after a special service, Mr A E **Glassey** JP, a deacon of the church and MP for Poole (1932-36), welcomed the Mayor and Mayoress of Poole, Councillor and Mrs H C R **Ballam**, together with the visitors including the Rural Dean, Canon R Creed **Meredith** representing the Deanery and Council of Christian Churches; Reverend Charles **Haig**, Moderator of the Western Province of the Congregational Union; Reverend T D **Watkins**, Chairman of the Dorset Congregational Association and representatives of the Skinner Street, Longfleet, Hamworthy, Lytchett and Wareham Congregational Churches.

The Mayor spoke of the esteem in which Reverend Walter **Dickinson** was held by a wide circle of responsible people in the life of the Borough, and tributes were paid to him by representatives of Poole Education Committee, Dorset Congregational Churches, Poole Free Church Council and Bournemouth Congregational Fraternal. Mr A J (Jack) **Hicks** spoke on behalf of the deacons and congregation and referred to his own family's long connection with the church started by his father, the late Herbert W **Hicks** headmaster of Branksome Heath School.

Throughout his Ministry at Parkstone, Reverend Walter **Dickinson** was much helped by his wife Daisy, who died in 1970, and their companion Miss Hilda **Skelton**. When he retired he married a member of the Church, Edna **Bonner**, whom he had first met over 20 years earlier as a Youth Club member. She later became the youngest lady deacon in the history of the Church. After their marriage they lived in Bournemouth where Edna was Deputy Headmistress to the Girls Grammar School, but following her retirement they returned to live in Parkstone and resume involvement within the Church.

Some of the many people who have given freely of their time and talents to Parkstone Congregational Church are Mr David **Haig**, who was Church Secretary for over 20 years until 1993, and his wife Christine; and Mr Ernest **Lukey**, a senior elder, who was Sunday School Superintendent for several decades, and his wife Megan, who celebrated their Diamond Wedding with a service at the Church on Sunday 23rd April 1995.

Reverend Norman **Cave** and Reverend Leonard **Garland** followed Walter **Dickinson**, and in 1972 the church became part of the United Reformed Church of England and Wales. Since then membership has declined, especially in the younger age groups, but the church continues to serve the local community and in recent years became a member of the ecumenical group *'Poole East Churches'*. The church spearheaded the appointment of a Free Church Chaplain for Bournemouth University by donating a third of its Centenary Gifts, nearly £500, to set up a fund to support such a Ministry and to the delight of the Parkstone church *'Free Churches in Bournemouth, Poole and surrounding areas'* responded to this challenge with just such an appointment in April 1994.

Reverend David **Bending**, who became Minister in July 1990, together with the care of Skinner Street and Longfleet, relinquished the Parkstone church at the end of 1993; and in 1995 Reverend Bryan **George**, retired chaplain of Westminster School in London, was appointed as part-time Minister at the Parkstone United Reformed Church.

The nine Elders in 1955 are Christine and David **Haig**, S E H **Lukey**, Miss Jean **Wilson**, Arthur **Green**, Mrs Kathleen **Jones**, Clifford **Hawes**, Jim **Campbell** Treasurer and Edna **Dickinson**.

Salterns Road Methodist (Wesleyan) Church

Salterns Road Methodist (Wesleyan) Church stands on the corner with Wessex Road, and in early 1995 the Minister was Reverend John **Hainsworth** MA BD.

The date of 1865 that can be seen on the outside of the present church refers, not to that building but to the original church. In 1900/1901 it was replaced, on an adjacent site, by the larger building still in use today. The original structure was kept in use until 1978 before being demolished, and in 1993 an extension was added to serve as a church hall following six years of fund raising.

Parkstone Methodist/Wesleyan Church - Late 1950's
Back row from left: Fred Ballam, Mr Thorne, Sidney Taylor, Len Newbold, Alfred Power, Charlie Offier, Arthur Bottomley
Middle row: Myrtle Bond, Iris Evernden, Winnie Offier, Aileen Bottomley, Jeanne Bottomley, Linda Speight, Annette. Bottomley, Valerie Power. Sitting: Mrs Brown (organist/pianist), Mrs Irene Taylor (choir mistress) and Margaret Norman
Courtesy: Iris Evernden

It is part of The Methodist Church Poole Circuit which covers Broadstone, Wareham and Lytchett Matravers as well as six in the Poole area. Minutes of Trustees Meetings, Account Books and Pulpit Notice Books for the Salterns Road church are deposited in the Dorset Record Office in Dorchester. The interior of the church contains an interesting ceramic font with grey stand and blue dish, which was created, it is believed, by the Poole School of Art. It commemorates Miss E **Sargent**, organist 1953-57, who was a very small lady who could apparently play absolutely anything and the more black notes there were the better she liked it!

After the 2nd World War an electric motor was installed for the organ, which until that time had been hand pumped by Mr Cyril **Dacombe**. For many years red serge curtains screened the organ but these were replaced soon after the war with a memorial screen of light oak and stained glass in remembrance of Geoffrey **Knight** - given by his parents, who were drapers in Station Road. Their son served in the RAF and was killed in 1943.

The preaching/reading desk commemorates William Talbot **Chinchen** and family, 1966; and a recent new organ was acquired by fund raising.

Several years ago the old wooden forms used by the congregation were sold to someone in the USA and replaced by more comfortable seating arrangements. The church was delighted that in America signs of woodworm are most sought after!

Iris **Evernden** has long been associated with the Salterns Road Methodist Church for she started attending Sunday School there in 1936; helped with the under 8's in the Primary section, assisted with the Girls' Brigade for ten years until it was disbanded in 1976, and was a member of the choir. She still continues her involvement with the various church groups today.

Describing the church community as thriving but small with a good fellowship, she said *'our congregation numbers between 40 and 50 and we have a ten-strong choir; and the two regular groups - Salty Fellowship and Tuesday Group Network are well attended'.*

The Salty Fellowship, a house group, was started in 1986 by Brian and Angela **Daniels** in their home in Mentone Road and is now run by Iris **Hulme**. The Tuesday Network is the umbrella of all the women's groups which includes Bright Hour, Sisterhood, Women's Works and Women's Fellowship within the Wesleyan Church.

Recalling her early days in the choir, Iris **Evernden** remembers regular visits to sing in country churches. *'We used to take members of our own congregation with us and everyone enjoyed themselves. On one occasion the music for the choir had been left behind on a kitchen table, but luckily the organist had hers and we managed to complete our repertoire without mishap. I remember the church at Horton Heath near Cranborne still used oil lamps - this was probably in the 1960s.*

'When I first started at the Sunday School in 1936 it was run by Mr Reginald Power; later his daughter Aileen took over and between them they gave almost 50 years service to the Sunday School'.

The photographs with this chapter were lent to me by Iris **Evernden** and in many instances she found it difficult to give me the Christian names of the people involved. In these days of total informality and overall use of Christian names, it is probably hard to realise that it is not so long ago that Christian names were not generally used, and individuals were described as Mr, Mrs or Miss with perhaps their initials.

One last memory from Miss **Evernden** relates to food. It seem that Cadman's the bakers (now Bennett's) delivered fancy cakes to households on a Saturday and one was able to choose from the tray the cakes you fancied for eating on Sunday.

Choir and members of congregation - Parkstone Methodist/ Wesleyan Church 1968.
Courtesy: Iris Evernden

III

Education

ⓘ *Parkstone School / Parkstone Grammar / Ashley Cross Girls School 1905-1988*

Parkstone Grammar School celebrated its 90th anniversary on 24th January 1995. Although now situated beyond Fleetsbridge in Sopers Lane, Poole, the school was once a distinctive feature in Commercial Road at Ashley Cross, with its decorative facade and splendid carved oak doors.

Initially a fee paying church school for boys and girls, it became Parkstone Grammar School in 1934 when taken over by Dorset County Council. Three years later the boys transferred to their own Poole Grammar School at Seldown, and so two single sex establishments were created. In 1961 Parkstone Grammar moved to a purpose built school in Sopers Lane and the original building in Commercial Road became the Ashley Cross School for Girls until 1987 when the 420 pupils merged with the Seldown School for Boys to form Ashdown School at Canford Heath.

The Ashley Cross School buildings remained empty and desolate for several years, but were eventually demolished and the site developed with Council rented accommodation in 1994/5.

The Early 1900s

It all began in the early 1900s. The original building was not designed as a school but as a Church House for meetings of all kinds and for educational purposes.

St Peter's Church used rooms at St Peter's School in Parr Street on a regular basis and it appears that use was already made of the Working Mens Club (Parkstone Technical Institute) at the 'Welcome Coffee House' on a casual footing. After the completion of the new St Peter's Church building in September 1901, the need for a Church House became more and more urgent but the church coffers were empty. A committee was formed to look into the matter and one of the members was Mr William Ernest **Brennand** of *'Belmont'* in Parkstone.

This horse drawn transport is travelling along Commercial Road towards Poole. In the background is The Parade. Parkstone School is just out of the photograph on the left.
Date is probably early 1900's.
Courtesy: Mrs Mary Fraser, née Moss

A local solicitor, church warden and Town Councillor, Mr **Brennand** saved the situation by offering to finance the project. It was not known at that time how he proposed to do this but later it became evident that rental from the row of shops built at the same time and called 'The Parade' would provide the necessary income.

Regarding the Church House, the Parkstone Reminder dated 24th September 1904 states -

The result is the very handsome and commodious building on the Parade, which Mr Brennand has erected at his own risk, so adjusting its financial conditions and resources that it may be held by Vicar and Churchwardens at the small yearly rental of seventy five pounds, to be raised by them by means of subscriptions from such parishioners as appreciate the public advantages to be gained by the possession of so admirable a centre of Parish life and work'.

Designed by the architect Mr Walter **Andrew** of Alton Chambers, Station Road, Church House was built by Burt and Vick with the carving on the front doors being carried out by a Mr Joseph **Pearcy**, uncle of Audrey **Pearcy** who gave freely of her time to St Peter's Church.

Only 43 years of age when he died, Mr Walter **Andrew's** work was carried out on the Wimborne estates and included a number of residences at Parkstone, schools and other buildings in the Bournemouth District. His death was reported in **The Builder'** and the East Dorset Herald dated 6th April 1911, mentioned his association with the public life of Poole as a Councillor, and Sheriff in 1890. He was a member of Amity Lodge; and was remembered as an enthusiastic sportsman, having played in county cricket matches for both Hampshire and Dorset.

Mr W E **Brennand's** great interest lay in education and he believed that Parkstone should have its own Secondary School. He, therefore, built a school behind the existing Church House calling it The Colet Institute after Dean Colet, who was Dean of St Paul's at the beginning of the 16th C and the pioneer of *'secondary education'*. This additional building was the forerunner of many and varied extensions which later caused the school to be described as *'a rabbit warren'*. The Colet Institute was offered to the Education Committee for use as a grammar school by Mr **Brennand** but his offer was declined; and he decided to open his own school.

The Governors, Mr W E **Brennand** (Chairman), The Venerable the Archdeacon of Dorset, The Reverend Canon **Dugmore** Vicar of Parkstone, Mrs Dawson **Damer**, Mrs W E **Brennand**, Mr T K **Ingram** and Mr A **Kelly**, issued a Prospectus at the end of 1904. Providing for pupils of both sexes from the age of nine upwards, the school was described as being situated within five minutes walk from Parkstone railway station and from the tram lines between Poole and Bournemouth. The fees were £1.10.0. per term for children under 12, and £2.2.0. for those over 12 with a reduction of 10% for each pupil of the same family, other than the first.

The Staff

The first (and only) headmaster was Reverend E Stanley **Moss**, and when the school opened on 24th January 1905 he had only one assistant, Miss **Beale**, whose salary was £75 per annum. There were 14 pupils on that first day, by the end of the second year the number had risen to 98 and four years later the school was full with 150 pupils. This despite the fact that at the time many people declared that there was no room for another secondary school in the borough and that it was bound to fail.

A school magazine was printed for the first time in December 1908, only three years after the foundation of the school. The object of the magazine was to provide *'a record of school life and activities'*, and could be bought for 6d (2^1/$_2$p) per copy.

The headmaster stayed at the school until his retirement in 1937, and at the Jubilee Reunion in January 1955 several former pupils spoke of his dedication to the school in times of great difficulty and referred to his powerful influence on their lives. A former Head Girl painted a vivid word picture of Reverend Stanley E **Moss** -

'He was an Anglican clergyman in the High Church tradition, of medium height, and everything about him except his clerical collar, was black: from his black suit to his black hair and his bushy black eyebrows, under which were a pair of shrewd piercing eyes which would sometimes light up in a twinkle of amusement, especially when he spoke to young children or slyly pulled the leg of an over-earnest prefect. When he addressed the School, he scarcely ever raised his voice above a quiet conversational tone, and yet, somehow we never failed to hear what he said, though to do so meant straining one's ears and sitting without moving a muscle.'

Up to 1912, a year in which the Inter-School Challenge Shield was won and many academic distinctions gained, the school prospered. But that year saw the beginning of grave financial burdens which were not resolved until 1934 after the school had been taken over by the County Council. In the previous year, 1911, St Peter's Church refused to take up the option of purchasing Church House, and when in July 1912 Mr W E **Brennand**, Chairman of the Governors and virtual founder of the school, died suddenly whilst chairing a School Board meeting, it was found that the building was heavily mortgaged. Apparently income from the adjacent shops had proved inadequate.

The financial problems did not go away and the school struggled on. The County was again approached with a view to taking it over and again refused. Herbert **Carter**, the then Chairman of the Education Committee wrote in his autobiography *'I Call to Mind'* -

'On the following day, the late Mr John Dyson and I looked over the premises of the Parkstone (Grammar) School with a view to its being taken over by the County. We spent some time over the job and decided that the building, which was not designed for a school, was most unsuitable and would need large sums spent on it to make the proposition practicable. Later our judgement was disregarded and the school taken over (1943), but it remains today a first-rate school in spite

of, and not because of, the lay-out and construction of the buildings.'

The First World War 1914-1918 saw the departure of some of the masters on active service, but in spite of obvious difficulties academic work proceeded steadily and numbers continued to rise. The following editorial appeared in The Parkstonian December 1914 -

The thing uppermost in everyone's minds is the great European War. It is the greatest War in history, and the most terrible. And yet, whilst casting a shadow over everyone, it has caused people to help one another. At school we are trying to do our best to relieve the great distress which is prevalent everywhere. A subscription fund has been started and we have already sent a small sum to the Prince of Wales for his Relief Fund. The girls are knitting different articles for the sailors, and Mr Moss has very kindly given one of the Needlework lessons for this purpose. A number of Old Parkstonians are serving with the forces of our Country, and a list of their names will be found on another page'.

Improvements

In 1918 a fund raising campaign was launched to roof over the open courtyard between the buildings, and in 1922 the Great Hall was opened. At the same time, the shop next door to the school was taken in, originally to form the Preparatory department and later to serve as a cloakroom. For a short time they also used 59 Commercial Road, next door to the school, which later became the Education Office and Youth Employment Office.

The *'Great Hall'* was to prove extremely useful, both to the school and to the local Parkstone community, serving as the venue for large events and public meetings. A protest meeting was held there on 1st June 1933 against the proposal of the Bankes estate to grant to the Shell Bay Development Company permission to erect at South Haven - subject to a licence being granted by the Harbour Commissioners - a landing stage which all persons embarking or disembarking there would have to use on payment of a toll.

If the weather had been inclement on 20th May 1950 then the Great Hall would have been used for the presentation of the Honorary Freedom of the Borough to Olave, Lady **Baden-Powell** GBE Chief Guide to the World. As it was the weather was fine and the presentation took place in front of the cricket pavilion in Poole Park.

Taking advantage of the size of the Great Hall, the Poole Boy Scouts Association held their St George's Day Rally there in 1952 (the first since the end of the war in 1945) and again in 1953 and 1954.

County Ownership

The next important step came in 1934 when the County finally took over the buildings and it became known as Parkstone Grammar School. To the Headmaster this may well have been a mixed blessing, an enormous financial burden was lifted from his shoulders but at the same time he had to forego the denominational religious education which had always been a fundamental part of the school. Until his retirement in 1937 Reverend Stanley **Moss** continued to run the mixed school which he started in 1905 and to which he had devoted 32 years service.

Single Sex Schooling

In April 1937 Miss W M **Allen** from Grimsby High School was appointed Headmistress and for one term continued to run a co-educational school with a mixed staff. This was unheard of in those days and must have been difficult for Miss **Allen**. In the September pupils and staff were *'sorted out'*, boys and masters going to their own school in Poole and girls and mistresses staying in the Ashley Cross buildings, thus making two single-sex establishments.

An increase in the number of girls necessitated the addition of the new *'Wooden Wing'* and the gymnasium split horizontally and vertically to make two pairs of classrooms divided by folding screens known as *The Doubles'*. The Oaks, a pair of semi-detached houses in the grounds were converted into one building and became part of the school.

As the Second World War began in September 1939 Poole (a so-called *'safe region'*) became a reception area for London evacuees and numbers rose from under 300 in 1937 to 500 in the early 1940's. Air raids disrupted the normal life of the school as the siren sounded and everyone trooped down to the shelters. Many of the pupils naturally enjoyed these diversions, and it is a tribute to the war-time teachers that pupils continued to satisfactorily complete their education.

Staff, and senior girls during the holidays, became fire watchers which entailed a rota of night duty. This was a precautionary measure so that in the event of fires caused by enemy bombs or incendiaries, immediate action could be taken with buckets of sand and hose pipes.

Edna **Dickinson** (née Bonner), who was at the school 1938-1945 recalls the war-time years:

'We were too young to realise the full significance of the war and continued to live as normal a life as possible. We wore long sleeved overalls as uniform to protect our clothes - be they school clothes or otherwise

- and everyone had to carry a gas mask. Routine gas mask inspection interrupted lessons - all the more so if one could convince the member of staff that our own no longer fitted satisfactorily! Air raid warnings meant an immediate move to the shelters - the only time we were allowed to use the main front exit - with continuation of the lesson as far as possible. The sound of 'moaning minnie', as it was called, just as school ended was a real disaster. We tried to escape before being 'rounded up' into the shelters' but at the height of the war no-one was allowed on the streets during an air raid so there was no alternative.

Summer family holidays were non-existent then and the school's answer was a 'Holiday Term', the girls attending on a voluntary basis for such subjects as elocution, drama, First Aid and Household Hints. Special working autumn holidays took us into the heart of Dorset for potato picking; armed with sandwiches, pork pies or anything we could lay our hands on, we travelled by coach to the fields, returning in the evening exhausted but with some money in our pockets.

School lunches during the war left a lot to be desired - burnt custard and watery rice - left me with a life time aversion to milk puddings!

I used to cycle daily from Oakdale to Ashley Cross and recall that one morning we saw bombs dropping at the top of Castle Hill. Later in the war (June 1944) we stopped cycling, to watch in amazement, as planes filled the sky on their way to the D-Day Landings'.

Joan **Elford** 1942-48 has the following recollections of those years:

'I remember Miss Cowles reading to us in the air raid shelter - Silas Marner - Mill on the Floss, and singing together to while away the time. I remember the poor state of the building. There were always buckets to catch the water from the leaking roof and one year The Mayor, Alderman Bright, a portly man, came to speak and give the prizes. He walked down the Hall with Miss Allen, climbed the steps on to the platform and promptly fell through the rotten floor board. I remember the enjoyment of Guide camps with Miss Cowles and Miss Barnes. We were at camp in August of VJ year and were told hostilities had ceased. We walked to Swyre Head and watched all the bonfires lit along the coast, and then returned to hot cocoa'.

After the War

After the war it was Miss **Allen's** task to restore the school to some form of normality. Numbers continued to rise and,

as 59 Commercial Road was acquired by the Education Office, extensive alterations were carried out at *The Oaks'*. After 1947 the girls enjoyed the luxury of a canteen, all meals previously being eaten in the hall; and The Horsa Huts (rooms 25 + 26) were built.

A short distance away, at the North Road end of St Peter's Road and near the school playing fields, was a spacious Victorian house called *Torvaine'*. The Fire Service had recently vacated the building and it became an annexe to Parkstone Grammar and housed the Ashley Cross Girls for half a term before they were able to move into the main buildings. *Torvaine'* is now a private school - Eagle House, run by Mrs Joan **Rees**.

In 1953, the year in which Reverend E Stanley **Moss** died, it was discovered that the entire front of the building in Commercial Road was unsafe. With the school in session, all the sandstone front was taken out, including one wall of Miss **Allen's** room, and completely rebuilt. All that then remained of the original frontage was the decorative oak doors.

School Reunion

At the beginning of 1955 the school held a Jubilee Reunion and Commemoration. In the afternoon of Friday, 7th January the whole school assembled in the Hall to hear the brief history outlined by the Headmistress, Miss **Allen**, together with reminiscences of former pupils. A similar programme was carried out in the evening when the Hall was filled with Old Pupils and Staff, Governors, the Staff and Sixth Form. It was on this occasion that the Jubilee Fund was opened 'to give grants and loans to senior girls where need arises'. Contributions came from the school, old pupils and from parents and subsequently many girls have had cause to be grateful for the insight of those who inspired this Jubilee Fund.

Miss **Allen** had welcomed Mrs **Moss**, wife of the first Headmaster Reverend E Stanley **Moss** to the Jubilee Reunion, together with three members of the family - Barty, Osmund and Mary (Bernard sent a telegram from Johannesburg) and the next day, Saturday 8th January Reverend W H Osmund **Moss** preached the sermon for The Jubilee Service of Thanksgiving. This was held at St Peter's Church, conducted by the Vicar, Reverend H J **Coulson** with the lessons read by Canon **Archer** (Vice Chairman of the Governors) and the singing led by the School Choir. About 260 current girls attended and about 150 Old Pupils and friends.

In his sermon Reverend W H Osmund **Moss** mentioned the first Commemoration Day Service of the school held on Wednesday 27th January 1909, indicating that it was intended as an act of public thanksgiving to God for all past blessings, and a prayer for future guidance. He described a school as *'a miniature of human history, and therefore of the life of individuals: it is made up of joy and sadness, of triumph and suffering, of courage and weakness, of hope and disillusionment; and its greatness and our pride lie in these aspects of its life'*.

The Parkstone Grammar School Magazine for 1954-55 recorded that the Great Hall was redecorated in September 1954, the Annual School Service was held at St Peter's Church on 27th October, 1954 and the school was addressed by Miss **Reader Harris**, Headmistress of Sherborne School, at the Speech Day on 23rd November of that same year. The school play in that Jubilee year of 1955 was *'Cranford'*; and the School House names were Austen, Bronte, Cavell, Curie, Fawcett, Fry, Garrett-Anderson, Nightingale, Pankhurst, Slessor.

New Building

Before the war Parkstone Grammar had been promised a new building but it was not until 1958, Miss **Allen**'s 21st year, that a site in Sopers Lane was finally chosen and provision made in the County estimates. Due to the delay, Miss **Allen** did not, after all, take the school to their new building; she generously retired in December 1959 so that a new Head could make the preparations for the move. She did, however, lay the foundation stone in April 1960. Many tributes were paid to Miss **Allen** at her death in 1979, with person after person commenting on her wisdom, her kindly understanding and her Christian example.

In 1960 Miss N L **McGuinness** from Totnes High School became Headmistress and had the task of moving the school to the new premises; according to the Chairman of the Governors it was *'the greatest upheaval of all time'*. It had been anticipated that the move would take place during the summer but the work was behind schedule and although the new buildings were far from finished, the girls finally took possession of their new school in November 1961. On the first bus was a giant stuffed panda named *'Ashley'*, who became the school mascot and attended every function for many years.

The new Parkstone Grammar School at Sopers Lane was officially opened on 9th July, 1962 by the Right Honorable Sir David **Eccles**, KCVO, MP, Minister for Education. He was welcomed to the school by the Mayor, Alderman W T **Haskins**, and a short Service of Dedication was conducted by Reverend Canon G D **Archer**, Vice Chairman of the Board of Governors. Votes of thanks to Sir David were proposed by the Chairman of the Dorset County Education Committee, County Alderman J D **Chesterfield** and by the Head Girl, Sylvia **Dominey**. A vote of thanks to the Mayor was proposed by Mr L G **Adams**, Chairman of the Board of Governors and a former pupil of the school.

Carved oak doors of Parkstone School/Parkstone Grammar/ Ashley Cross Girls School, not long before demolition. Unfortunately, the doors were not saved for use elsewhere.

In 1976 Miss **McGuinness** retired and her place as Headmistress taken by Mrs C E **Birchett** from the Purbeck School.

The New Secondary School

We now leave Parkstone Grammar School in Sopers Lane to continue their own history and return to Ashley Cross to complete the last 26 years of the school buildings as home to the new secondary school, the first in Poole for 12 years.

Unable to move into their new school until the Parkstone Grammar girls had vacated the premises in November 1961 (instead of the beginning of term in September) the Ashley Cross Girls began work in the cramped conditions at *Torvaine'* with Miss G F **Ashurst** as Headmistress.

The school served the Canford Cliffs, Sandbanks, Lilliput, Branksome and Lower Parkstone areas and initially there were 130 girls within the 1st and 2nd year forms, the 2nd year pupils having come from other secondary schools.

They coped with many difficulties during those first few months in *'Torvaine'* - furniture had to be moved back and forth each day so that morning assembly could take place in the largest of the classrooms, and girls became adept at eating hot lunches on the sloping lids of classroom desks. No-one was allowed to be vigorous in their PE exercises in the attic because it was feared that the floor boards would collapse, and the staff themselves shared a minute staff room with almost standing room only.

Described as the *'School with the Red Stockings'*, the distinctive smart uniform of cherry red V neck pullovers with knee length socks to match, teamed with white blouses, navy blue skirts and blazers became a well known sight in Ashley Cross. In the early years an attractive peaked corduroy beret was also worn, at many different angles, but hatlessness soon came into fashion. The regulation all

Parkstone School at Ashley Cross under construction - early 1900's. The Parade (shops) to the right were built to help finance the school.

round pleated skirt eventually gave way to a skirt *'suitable for school'* and over the years this was interpreted as very short minis (with tights), very tight skirts and in the early 80's long full skirts, some with frills!

Once Parkstone Grammar pupils had vacated their old school in November 1961, the Ashley Cross girls set about moving into the Commercial Road buildings from *'Torvaine'* in St Peter's Road. Supervised by the then caretaker, Mr **Martin**, all the girls helped in the removal of books, stationery and small items of furniture. A pupil at that time wrote in the school magazine *'when I saw the school I fully agreed with the person who had likened it to a large rabbit warren; it was a peculiar building spread over quite a large area, with the buildings here and there. As soon as the books were unpacked, we were allowed to explore our unfamiliar surroundings, with everyone getting lost at least once.'*

Alterations and additions to the buildings continued over the next 20 years - two new rooms (31 + 32) were built on to the back of *The Oaks'*, two temporary classrooms (20 + 21) were put on the front lawn, and after a fire inspection all the attic rooms were closed to the girls and the library rehoused downstairs. In 1971 the school leaving age was raised to sixteen and the 5th Year Unit was built on what remained of the orchard between *The Oaks'* and the Wooden Wing and a rare medlar tree disappeared to make room for cars. In 1975 rooms 33 + 34 were taken over from St Peter's School and by 1977 room 35 was added to *The Oaks'* to cope with the increase from 90 to 140 girls in the 5th Year.

The task undertaken by Miss G F **Ashurst**, Headmistress until her retirement in 1974, was that of creating a new school, co-ordinating staff and pupils to produce a happy and secure atmosphere in which the girls could develop and flourish. The conditions under which the school operated within the *'rabbit warren'* were impractical but not insurmountable, and it seems that the very presence of those difficult circumstances encouraged the whole school to create their own spirit of endeavour.

Service to the Community

Staff and pupils worked together to create a badge for the new school. After research into the Ashley Cooper family tree from Wimborne St Giles and permission from Lady Lettice Ashley **Cooper**, the design was based on their Coat of Arms and incorporated a lion and a staff representing service to the community - thus commemorating the work of the 7th Lord Shaftesbury, 1801-1885. Mrs A **Quick** was responsible for the final design of the school badge, and school chose as their motto *'We Serve'*.

Miss M H **Mulraine** came to Ashley Cross Girls from Wareham Secondary in April 1965 and worked, as Deputy Head, with Miss **Ashurst** for nine years before herself becoming Headmistress in 1974.

Together with Miss Joy **Phillips**, Miss **Mulraine** was responsible for organising the Duke of Edinburgh Award Scheme in 1966. *'A weekend course in London filled us with enthusiasm and confidence, and we started with 30 enthusiastic and starry-eyed fourteen year olds. We all learned as we went along, made many mistakes, laughed a lot and, to our amazement, were able to hold a Gold Award presentation for our first three girls in April 1970'.*

Up until 1974 the policy of Dorset County Council had been that of appointing Heads from other schools so Miss **Mulraine** was the first Deputy Head in Dorset to be promoted within her own school. *'Miss Ashurst had created a unique atmosphere for the new school and I was able to provide continuity for the girls and the rest of the staff.'*

Birthday Celebrations

'As we knew the future of the school in its present buildings was uncertain we decided, in 1982, to celebrate its 21st birthday. This took the form of a wonderful reunion, attended by staff and girls covering every year from 1961 to 1982.'

'My Deputy Head was Mrs Audrey Quick, formerly Head of the Art Department, who had a tremendous rapport with the girls. The school had established a fine reputation for the quality of its Art; and Mrs Quick firmly believed that everyone had some creative talent and endeavoured to ensure that, on Open Day, every pupil had a piece of work on display.'

Immediately on her retirement from the school in 1983 Miss **Mulraine** began a 3 year course at Salisbury Theological College and, in 1986 was made Deaconess. In the following year, as the Anglican Church had now given its approval for the ordination of women, she was ordained as a Deacon, and became a non-stipendiary minister in the

Wareham Team and in charge of St Nicholas Church, Arne.

In June 1994, with 38 other women deacons, she was ordained as a priest in Salisbury Cathedral. As all clergy retire at the age of 70, she now continues a retirement ministry, as Priest-in-Charge, at St Nicholas, Arne.

Co-Education

September 1983 saw the arrival of the last headmistress. As with several of her predecessors, Mrs M **Snell** was to cope with a specific situation relating to the school, which in her case was the closure of Ashley Cross Girls School and the transition to the new mixed school at Canford Heath with boys from the Seldown school in Poole.

Completion of the building of the new Ashdown Secondary School, so named to retain something of the past of both establishments, was delayed so following the pattern set in 1961 when the new Parkstone Grammar building was not ready on time. 1987 should have seen everyone settling down into the new Canford Heath building but this did not happen until September 1988. During that last year both continued to operate as single sex schools, but Ashley Cross had, in addition, mixed classes for the 12 year olds with buses running to and fro between the schools.

During the school year 1986-7, the running of Ashley Cross Girls was left in the capable hands of the Deputy Head Mrs Pamela **Sleat**, who was Head of the Home Economics Department, whilst Mrs **Snell** concentrated on the forward planning for the new secondary school on Canford Heath.

'My task was to liaise with the architects of the new building, arrange the curriculum for what should have been the first year of the new school and appoint staff; and much of my time was spent travelling between the three schools'.

Many of Mrs **Snell's** memories of the last year of the Ashley Cross Girls School 1987-88 were of a practical nature regarding the physical disadvantages of the building. Through damp conditions the school had for many years been able to grow its own fungi, antiquated heating systems were unable to cope with the very cold weather conditions and ancient drains caused sewage problems from time to time. The October 1987 hurricane felled one of *The Oaks'*, blocking the staff car park, and a flood inside the school on New Year's Eve had Mrs **Snell** stopping the traffic in Commercial Road in an effort to locate the mains stopcock. Water poured down the main staircase and the temporary caretaker had no idea where to find the all important water tap inside the school! At one stage, a mummified owl was found behind a blocked fireplace. The bird's feathers were intact and presumably it had fallen down the chimney at some time in the past.

But despite the drawbacks of the building everyone, girls and staff alike, were sad to leave and past pupils always mention the happy atmosphere which prevailed.

In July 1988 the school closed, not just for the summer holidays, but for ever. To give the staff time to pack up at Ashley Cross and unpack at Ashdown, the school closed early in July thus giving the pupils an extra couple of weeks holiday. The Seldown boys school also closed earlier than usual for they had bulldozers and road engineers breathing down their necks waiting impatiently to get on with the building of the new Seldown Bridge.

Mrs **Snell**, having co-ordinated the move to Canford Heath, was appointed Head of the new Ashdown Secondary School; and her two Deputy Heads were Mr Clive **Cole** who had been Headmaster at Seldown and Mrs Pamela **Sleat** previously Deputy Head at Ashley Cross.

The school was officially opened by Princess Margaret in July 1989 and when Mrs **Snell** retired in 1990 her place as Head was taken by Mr Ashley **Pelligrini**.

Sarah **Clapcott** was in her 4th year (1st Year GCSE's) when the move took place. She recalls that the staff at the time were Mrs **Searle** (Miss **Guy**), RE and Music; Miss **Bray**, English; Miss **Francis**, PE; Mrs **Tripp**, Science; Mrs **Steel**, Geography and Humanities; Mrs **Wickens**, Child Development and Home Economics; Mrs **Dimbleby**, Needlework; Mrs **Winch**, Science; Miss **Bartlett**, Geography; Miss **Davis** and Miss **Davies**, one Science and other Mathematics; Mrs **Boyle**, English. There was apparently one male member of staff, but Sarah can neither remember his name nor the subject he taught!

'Complete chaos reigned in the school during that last year', she said. *'I remember that some of our lessons were held at Ashley Cross and some at Seldown, so much time was spent on bus journeys; it thoroughly disrupted my GCSE studies. Nevertheless, we were all rather excited at the prospect of starting at the new school in September'.*

With the closure of the school, a substantial part of the history of Ashley Cross disappeared for ever.

The celebrations at the beginning of 1995 of the 90th anniversary of Parkstone School/Parkstone Grammar included an exhibition of memories from past pupils; and it is intended to keep this collection of photographs and memorabilia in portfolio form at Parkstone Grammar School in Sopers Lane.

My particular thanks to Mrs Marion Watson, who allowed me unlimited access to her own research work on Parkstone School.

St Peter's School - a class in 1914
Courtesy: Ms Diane Evans

ⅱ *St Peter's School 1833-1988*

6th November 1895: *'Closed school this Wednesday until Monday, there being a Chrysanthemum Show this week in the school rooms'.*

This entry in the log book of St Peter's School in Parr Street (once Church Street) indicates the important part it played within the local community in those early days; and to many it was a sad day in 1988 when, not only St Peter's but the Ashley Cross Girls School closed their doors for ever. As a Grade II Listed building, St Peter's still stands in Parr Street, unlike the Ashley Cross Girls School, of which no trace is left.

A description by the Royal Commission on Historical Monuments states *'standing 80 yards SSW of St Peter's Church, of one storey with rendered brick walls and a slate-covered hipped roof, was built in the early 19th C and later extended to the rear. The front has four windows with pointed heads, and end porches'.*

St Peter's School is believed to be Dorset's oldest building to be continuously used as an educational establishment, and is acknowledged as the best remaining cob structure within the Borough of Poole. The cob built front wall - from Dorset clay, chalk and horse hair layered within timber shuttering - was in need of repair in 1992 and despite objections from the Society of Poole Men and English Heritage, Poole Councillors gave approval for the developers to replace half of the collapsed cob wall with concrete. Experts feel that the use of concrete blocks adjacent to the old cob wall will lead to difficult problems in the future.

Some records indicate that the Church of England elementary school was established in 1835 and that the present building was erected in 1838 with the aid of the Trust of Ledgard, but the plaque on the front of the school,

the original building, clearly states 1833. At that time Parr Street was called Church Street and the name changed between 1903 and 1911, presumably to commemorate the Parr family who had so much involvement with St Peter's Church. Over the years, extensions were added at the rear to cope with the increased number of pupils.

It appears that in 1861 the school received its first Government grant when it had one certified teacher and one pupil/teacher; in 1865 a Government report stated that the average pupil attendance was 42, and this figure had risen to 144 by 1874.

Listed in the 1890 Kelly's Directory as the National School (Church of England School) the entry states *'national, enlarged 1886 for 400 children; average attendance 114 boys, 69 girls and 51 infants; Walter Jesse Taylor master; Miss P Poolman mistress; Miss Emily Edith Farmer infants mistress'.*

Average attendance by 1903 had risen to 365 - 140 boys, 120 girls and 105 infants - with Mr **Taylor** still as headmaster, assisted by Miss Jesse Alice **Farmer** mistress, and Miss Kate Eliza **Williams** infants mistress.

The 1918 and 1939 Kelly's described St Peter's as an elementary school and in 1961 as a Voluntary Primary School (junior mixed and infants). Its last title before closure in 1988 was St Peter's Middle School, and the 108 pupils then merged with the others at the new Baden-Powell Middle School in Mill Lane, adjacent to what was once George **Jennings** South Western Pottery. The name was chosen to commemorate the close ties within this area with Lord **Baden-Powell** 1857-1941, Founder of the Boy Scouts.

Staff at St Peter's as it closed were Mrs Jackie **Jenkins**, Mrs Shauna **Savill**, Mrs Lyn **Way**, Mrs Daphne **Gibson** (Secretary), Miss Lesley **Adams**, Mrs Lyn **Foster**, Mr Malcolm **Hayward**, Mr Peter **Hough**, Miss Ann **Humphrey**, Mrs Gian **Tondeur**, with, it is believed, the last six transferring to the new Baden-Powell Middle School.

Headmaster at St Peter's for 14 years, Mr Roland **Rapkins** moved to Hamworthy School where he took over the Headship from Mr Norman **Murray**.

Closing Events

To mark the closing of the school in July 1988 a series of events were staged for the pupils, staff, parents and friends which included reunion evenings, a Thanksgiving Service in St Peter's Church on 20th July and a playground party for the children.

The Thanksgiving Service was conducted by Canon Reverend Peter R **Huxham** and a special programme printed for the occasion. These extracts from the reminiscences of a former pupil, Joanne **Williams**, give an indication of the happy atmosphere created within the school and echoed in comments from other past pupils -

'St Peter's is a very nice school. When I first came, Katie and Nicola looked after me. They showed me where I should sit and where the hymn books were. I made more friends through the weeks, I made friends with Alison, Samantha and Annette. I liked games and English I enjoyed a lot. I wasn't so good at maths. I liked the school meals I made friends with Janine we became best friends. The teachers at St Peter's are very, very nice. I've learnt tons more things than I used to know. I like the Deputy Head he is very funny. But sometimes he can be a bit angry. The headmaster is calm and quiet. I like him as well. St Peter's is a quiet, small school and I like it a lot.'

A Part of the Community

Naturally, the school had very close connections with St Peter's Church with pupils attending weekday services on All Saints' Days and Ascension Day and taking part in processions through the streets. Some of the boys sang in the church choir and one remembers that the going rate for singing at weddings and funerals was one shilling (5p).

In the 1930/1940's the front part of the school was for the girls with the boys at the rear and infants at the side of the alleyway. David **Lawrence** remembers the stump of a large tree in the front playground, which was reputed to be even older than the original building, and said that Ascension Day was always a day off school after attendance at the church service. He also mentioned that Penn Hill Avenue was then a profitable place for carol singing.

Although a lady from Bristol, Peggy **Wright** née Hayward, remembers buying a pennyworth of chips from the fish and chip shop on the corner of Commercial Road and Britannia Road (now demolished) and faggots and peas from Mrs **Genge**, who ran a butcher's shop, her favourite shop was Mrs **McGrath's** sweet shop in Parr Street (now a betting shop) where she bought her bag of chocolate stars for one halfpenny.

Among the staff remembered by past pupils in the 1930/1940's are Miss **Best**, Mr **Carter**, Miss **Ruth**, Miss **Langlois**, Miss **Fielding**, Miss **Bean**, Miss **Rogers**, Miss **Matthews**, Mr **Jefferies**, Miss **Rutter**, Mrs **Whitfield**, Miss **Alford**, Mr **Watkins**, Mr **Johnston** and Miss **Flowers**. Headmasters not forgotten are Mr **Galloway**, Mr Tommy **Rice**, Mr **Sayer** and Mr P **Brooks**, who it appeared was known for sending a boy to Bonnetts (where Vineys now stands in Commercial Road) to get a nice bloater for his tea!

One old boy of St Peter's School in the 1940's went on to take a full part in the civic and public life of the town. Denis

Gooding was Mayor of Poole for 1975/6, has held various appointments within the Borough of Poole Scout Council and has close connections with St John's Ambulance Brigade. His Charity Appeal in his Mayoral year was divided between the Scouts and Alderney Hospital, and the Denis **Gooding** Scout Centre in Layton Road, Upper Parkstone commemorates that involvement.

As well as recalling that Alderman Herbert **Carter** attended speech days and gave out prizes, he has retained the memory of the school outing to London when he lost his shirt on the return train journey, and of visiting the soup kitchens in Chapel Road - many families in the early 1930's lived in extreme poverty and some parents were unable to buy sufficient food for their children.

Denis **Gooding** walked the three miles from Newtown and back each day, and spoke of the thrill of hearing the siren which signified the turn-out of the fire engine from the fire station between Salterns Road and Britannia Road (now the library). "All the boys would rush to the railings to catch a glimpse of the splendid vehicle with solid tyres, and the firemen in their brass helmets. A policeman, from one of the police houses in Salterns Road, would hop on to the fire engine as it emerged from the double doors which faced Commercial Road".

Every child at school then had one third of a pint of milk (free) to drink with a straw during the morning break, and Denis **Gooding** used to collect the crates of milk from a dairy opposite the school in Parr Street.

Before the advent of the National Health Service (pre 1948) school children were given free medical care and dental treatment at central clinics. One such clinic was off Market Street in Poole and the St Peter's pupils would travel on the trams which ran along Commercial Road.

Other memories from past pupils mention two sweet shops in Parr Street and a bakery famous for their doughnuts; also Barrett's Riding Stables which were on the other side of the road. In his bowler hat, breeches and well-polished gaiters Mr F P **Barrett** would be seen driving his pony and trap; and upwards of 15 horses were kept for the use of the young ladies at Sandecotes (now Uplands) School.

Parr Street was an interesting little community with the terraced cottages, the school and the church, two pubs - The Bull next to the school and The Bricklayers Arms - **Beeney**, watchmaker and jeweller; a milliner; mens hairdresser; bootmaker F C **Hall**; antique shop; Parkstone Conservative Club; **Wilsons** the builder and Parkstone Motor and Cycle Co (forerunner of Parkstone Motor Co in Station Road).

In the early 1960's, the business of Parrs Quality Confectionery Limited was to be found at 49/51, the previous occupier of which had been the Head Office of the Dorset Dairies Direct Milk Supply Limited. Started soon after the end of the Second World War, near Bournemouth Central railway station, the company initially produced potato crisps before expanding into boiled sweets and then lettered rock, and are now to be found in Alder Road. Many people remember the factory in Parr Street with its white walls; and one lady had a friend who worked there when crisps were the majority product - apparently on a Friday afternoon, the workers were allowed to take home with them as many crisps as they could cram into one bag!

St Peter's School
Palm Procession to St Peter's Church. From left: Daniel Nothan, Robert Price on Nimrod the donkey, David Holdroyd and Stephen White. 2nd April 1981.
Courtesy: Mrs Elsie Murray.

Outside St Peter's School July 1988 - staff and pupils, before the closure.
It is thought that the following staff are in the photograph - Roland Rapkins Headmaster, Miss Lesley Adams, Mrs Lynn Foster, Mr Malcolm Hayward, Mr P Hough, Miss Ann Humphrey, Mrs Jackie Jenkins, Mrs Shauna Savill, Mrs Gian Tondeur, Mrs Lyn Way, Mrs Daphne Gibson Secreatry.
Photographer: H Eckardt of Sturminster Newton.
Courtesy: Christopher Luxford.

To celebrate the 150th Anniversary of St Peter's School in 1983, a Summer Fayre was held during June in Parkstone Park. For the first time in living memory the Park was transformed into a village green with all the attendant games, stalls and entertainment. It was so successful that St Peter's Church have continued to organise a similar event each year.

Extracts from the school log books, indicate some of the difficulties and tragedies of late Victorian times. In March 1887 a child died from whooping cough, January 1890 one died from diptheria and a 5 year old girl Maud **Kedy** was tragically knocked down by a horse as she left the school in 1889.

Severe weather sometimes kept the attendance figures down - the school closed on the afternoon of 15th March 1877 due to snow and wind, *"attendance still very low owing to the bad weather conditions"* on 17th February 1888 and a month later *"there was a heavy fall of snow, only 20 children attended; registers not marked all day"*.

There were occasionally other reasons for absentee children, for on 6th July 1887 *"the Jubilee rejoicings on Kinson Heath have affected the attendance all day but more especially this afternoon when only 52 were present"*.

The listed building which served for 155 years, until 1988, as St Peter's School stood empty for a short while after the children left. In 1995 the front part was being used as office accommodation and the rear as a snooker club. Local residents were apprehensive when planning application was made for this last use, but it seems that peaceful co-existence has been achieved.

Buckholme Towers School

'Education through Happiness, Happiness through Education' is the motto of Buckholme Towers School, Commercial Road/Glenair Avenue. The motto was chosen by founder, Mrs Dorothy **Murray**, when in 1939 she opened the school in her own Pearce Avenue home, primarily to educate her son and daughter. The name of Buckholme Towers was taken from Mr **Murray's** ancestral home in Scotland, now a derelict castle with haunted dungeons.

An Independent Day School for Girls and Boys, from the age of three to twelve years, the school has used the present premises since the early 1940's, with considerable extensions and rear entrance in 1959, and became a Charitable Trust in 1963. Mrs **Murray** was succeeded as Principal by Mrs Hazel **Boyd** in 1971, and on her retirement in 1985 Mrs D **Stacey** took over until 1994, when the Governors appointed Mrs C B M **Westhead** as Head Teacher.

There are four Life Members and four elected Members of the Board of Governors with Mrs Ruth **Goulden**, daughter of the late founder, and Mrs Hazel **Boyd** as two of the Life Governors. Mr Peter **Hartles** is the Chairman.

Following the National Curriculum, pupils at Buckholme Towers are encouraged, in the small classes, to fulfil their potential in all areas of school life and to develop lively and enquiring minds. The children have the opportunity of understanding the importance and philosophy of Christian values, and each class regularly leads a School Assembly, in which parents are often invited to participate. The school supports many charitable institutions and encourages personal involvement from the pupils. The uniform is green and grey, and caps and hats are worn up to the age of eight.

Second World War

Air raids during the early part of the Second World War (1939-1945) meant that many lessons were interrupted, and Ruth **Goulden** remembers spending a lot of time under the stairs; also of seeing a German pilot parachuting on to the railway line just below Parkstone Station. Later in the war the house next door was used as billet for American Servicemen - the children welcomed their presence for they were given oranges and chocolate, items which were in very short supply in Great Britain at that time.

Modern Times

Headmistress for 14 years, Mrs Hazel **Boyd** recalls that there were 80 pupils in 1971 and this figure had doubled when she retired in 1985. *'Our Speech Days were held in the Great Hall of Parkstone Grammar School, which was on the opposite side of Commercial Road, and we held up the traffic for the children to cross the road. Our Sports Days were held in Poole Park, swimming lessons were at the Sandbanks Hotel in their indoor pool and pupils were able to learn to play tennis at the Canford Cliffs Hotel on Wednesday afternoons (Jimmy Cooper may be remembered as the licensee at the time)'.*

When Mrs **Boyd** retired in 1985 there were 18 staff, and in particular she remembers Miss **Matthews** and Mrs **Short**, wife of Bernard C **Short**, once Borough Librarian and author of several historical books on Poole.

On Tuesday, 15th March 1994, the then Mayor of Poole, Councillor **Grant-Braham**, paid an early morning visit to the school and joined the children for their morning Assembly. The younger children formed a guard-of-honour to greet him as he arrived, wearing his full regalia, accompanied by his wife the Mayoress, and his Mace Bearer. In Assembly the children were very interested in the lively description of his work, he history of his robes and chain of office, and the account of his recent walk through the Channel Tunnel in aid of charity. Before he left, the Mayor was presented with a *'pot of gold'* collection of small change the children had made as a contribution towards the money raised by the Tunnel Walk for the Childrens Society.

In 1995, the school has 150 pupils with a staff of 25 which includes Teaching Assistants, Specialist and Extra-Curricular Teachers. At the age of eleven or twelve, the children transfer to many different senior schools - State, Grant-maintained, Independent or Grammar.

1994 - Mayor of Poole Councillor Bruce Grant-Braham and his wife visit Buckholme Towers School.
Photographer: Rosenfeld Photography

IV

~~Municipal Buildings~~

ⓘ *Former Municipal Buildings &* *Fire Station/Parkstone Library*

Originally, the public affairs of Poole were conducted from a building (Old Guildhall) in Fish Street, until The Guildhall in Market Street was erected in 1761. The Municipal Buildings at Ashley Cross were built in 1900, and in 1932 the New Municipal Buildings, now Poole's Civic Centre, were opened by the Earl of Shaftesbury.

The following report is taken from papers in possession of Parkstone Library at Ashley Cross:

The Early History of The Municipal Buildings and Public Reading Room at Ashley Cross, Parkstone

'The Municipal Buildings at Ashley Cross were originally built by Poole Corporation in 1900 as a fire station and Corporation depot.

'It appears that as early as 1874 the Poole Town Council passed a Resolution "that a fire engine and all the necessary adjuncts should be kept in a central part of Parkstone". It was not until 11th July 1893, however, after several serious fires in Parkstone, that the Town Council decided to buy ground for a depot that would house the fire station.

'The site chosen by the Town Council was known as "Parkstone Green" and according to some of the older inhabitants of the area, was once the site of a "blind-house" or "village pound". Several residents were disappointed in this choice not only because of its limited size and awkward shape but also because it was one of the few remaining open spaces in central Parkstone.

'By February 1899 the scheme awaiting the approval of The Local Government Board provided for more than a fire station. It was hoped that it would incorporate a room for the use of committees and officials of the Borough. Mr Leonard Browne, of Castle Hill Parkstone, suggested that this room might also serve as a public reading room. There would be a public clock on the outside of the building, living rooms

for the caretaker and stalls for the fire engine horses. The general public opinion in Parkstone regretted the fact that it was impossible to incorporate a police station on the same site due to its limited size.

'At a Local Government Board Inquiry at Poole Guildhall on Tuesday January 24th 1899, the Town Clerk announced that it would cost £2,000 to provide the public offices and depot at Parkstone and that the Council had approved the plans. These plans provided a Board Room, fire station, sheds for two water vans, steam roller, carts and stores, a mess room for the men, a four-stall stable, an infirmary for the horses, and a harnesss room. The upper part of the building was for the caretaker's use comprising of living room, kitchen and three bedrooms. The building was to be in the Tudor style, built of red brick with stone dressings and featuring a clock facing the main road.

'The Town Clerk then specified that the Board room would be used for committee meetings or similar purposes but it was not proposed to hold Council meetings at Parkstone.

'Three months later in the 'Poole Guardian' of April 22nd, there was an article concerning the "Needs and Desires of Parkstone" in which were several comments on the planned Municipal depot. There had apparently been suggestions that the building might have been designed on a larger scale to incorporate a drill hall (which could also be used for concerts etc), a coffee tavern and a reading room, which would be open from 10am to 10pm. Also envisaged was the possibility of the reading room eventually becoming a free library, since the library at Poole was some distance away and the reference library there had rather limited opening hours.

Building Commences

'By July 1899, the building work was progressing under Mr H F J Barnes, the architect and Mr W J Cross, the building contractor. The corner stone was laid on Friday 14th July 1899 without ceremony much to the disappointment of the people of Parkstone who had waited for many years for a depot which would not only provide a telephone line to Poole but also a meeting place for borough committees concerned with Parkstone matters. The rest of the building was completed without any problem, except an oversight in the original design concerning the clock tower, which had to be raised above the adjacent roofs to render the clock face more visible.

The Official Opening

'The opening of the Municipal Buildings was planned for April 23rd 1900, St Georges Day, and the Mayor invited the children of the two public elementary schools in Parkstone to a tea in the afternoon. During the opening ceremony the Mayor announced that the Town Council had decided to allow the use of the ground floor room as a public reading room when it was not required for municipal affairs.'

The following report on the inauguration of The Buildings was taken from the "Parkstone Reminder" for 28th April 1900:

'Parkstone was decidedly **en fête** on Monday afternoon. The new Municipal Buildings at Ashley Cross had the Union Jack floating from the tower, and there was a large display of bunting in various directions. A marquee had been erected in Oaklands Road opposite the new building, and was arranged drawingroom-wise within. Here the Mayoress, with some of her guests, awaited the civic procession, which started at three o'clock from S. Peter's Schools, preceded by the Poole Town Band, in the following order, the Mayor, Aldermen and Councillors wearing their official and the clergy their academical robes.

'The Mayor (Councillor J A Cocker), Rev J A Lawson (the Mayor's Chaplain), the Sherriff (Councillor Walter Andrew), Aldermen H Farmer, W H Yeatman, and C J Woodford, Councillors C Carter, G Curtis, W Marston, T K Ingram, W Wheeler, Dr W Hooper Masters, H Saunders, G Bush, E Norrish, G W Green, J A Hawkes, W J Burden and H G B Frampton, Mr J H Salter Dickinson (Town Clerk), Mr J Elford (Borough Surveyor), Mr E J Conway J P (Borough Coroner), Mr P E L Budge (Clerk to the Justices), Mr J A Robson (Borough Treasurer), Mr W J Bacon (Lighting Inspector), Mr R Smith, jun (Sanitary Inspector), Dr J R Philpots, JP, Dr W Turner, JP, Mr J Mowlam (Harbour Commissioner), Mr W B Wadham (Collector of Dues), Mr Turner, the Town Sergeants (Messrs George Squibb and Samuel Venables), the Town Crier (Mr A James), Mr F F Wallis (Clerk of the Works), the Police Force (under the command of Deputy Chief Constable Hains, the Vicar, Canon Evans, Canon Usherwood, Rev J Salter Barrett, Rev C M Gane, and Messrs A Kelly and E Ferraby (Churchwardens).

'On the arrival of the procession at the Marquee, the Borough Surveyor, Mr Elford, presented the keys of the buildings to the Mayoress, who proceeded to open the great doors; and the large ground floor room being entered, the Mayor called upon the Vicar to read a Prayer, which was as follows-

'Almighty Lord God, Supreme Ruler of the kingdoms of this world, Whose Will it is that good order and right government shall prevail in every part of it: We Thy servants beseech thee to bless this undertaking, and to grant that these buildings may in their use promote the well-being of the inhabitants of this place. That we and all our fellow subjects of this Kingdom and Empire, may live true Christian lives in Thy fear, in loyal obedience to our Sovereign Lady the Queen, and in peace and charity one with another. Through Jesus Christ our Lord; to Whom, with Thee and the Holy Spirit, be all honour and glory, now and for ever. Amen.

'This done, the Mayoress declared the buildings open, saying it gave her great pleasure to accede to the request which had been made to her that she should open those buildings on the day of our patron Saint, S. George. She had much pleasure therefore in declaring that building and the adjoining premises open for municipal and other public purposes.

'Mr Alderman Farmer then proposed a vote of thanks to the Mayoress.

'He said that he had a pleasing duty to perform, and that was to propose that the best thanks of the Town Council, the inhabitants of Parkstone, and the Borough of Poole at large be given to the Mayoress for her kindness in coming there that day and formally declaring open, as she had done so gracefully that afternoon, the municipal buildings in which they were assembled. On such occasions as the present they were apt to be a little retrospective, but he hoped that anything he might say would not hurt anybody's feelings or that he should tread on anybody's toes. His remembrance of Parkstone went back to the time when there was no place of worship at all there, but almost so, as S. Peter's Church was the first building for the glory of God erected in that part of the Borough and before Parkstone was a part of the Borough. In the year 1833 there was a wave of church building enthusiasm passing over the town of Poole, and not only S. Peter's at Parkstone, but S. Mary's at Longfleet, and S. Paul's at Poole, were all built about the same year. Since then other places of worship had been erected both in connexion with the Church of England and other denominations, and one of the last things that the Town Council did at their meeting on Friday was to pass plans for the erection of a new Wesleyan Chapel not very far from that spot where they were assembled. There had been a Wesleyan Chapel in Parkstone for some time, but not large enough for the requirements of the place, and a more commodious one was about to be erected. As far as religious matters were concerned there had, therefore, been great progress, and he hoped it would continue. With all the privileges with which Parkstone was surrounded the people ought to be good, and no doubt they were. At the time to which he had referred (1833) Parkstone was not a part of the Borough, and about that period great events occurred in the history of this country. One was the passing of the Reform Act, another was the introduction of the Poor Law Bill, then the emancipation of the slaves, and after that came the Municipal Corporation Reforms Bill, by which Parkstone, Longfleet, and Hamworthy became parts of the Borough of Poole, and had remained so ever since. Parkstone was a very small place then, and was tacked on to one of the wards of Poole, but the place had grown so rapidly that, through the exertions of the Town Council, a scheme was brought forward and carried whereby the representation of the Borough was more equally divided, and the responsibilities distributed. Now they at Parkstone had their own representatives on the Town Council, but he hoped they would never forget that they represented not only Parkstone but the whole of the borough. He knew that it was very difficult sometimes to do so, but he hoped they would strive to the end. Having alluded to the natural beauties and the surroundings of Parkstone, Alderman Farmer concluded by expressing the hope that the place would go on prospering, and that the Council would have plenty of plans brought before them for the extension of the buildings in that part of the Borough.'

The Rector of Poole seconded the vote, and said:

'He thought it a happy circumstance that he was permitted to join in thanking a lady on that auspicious day, for if he had read history right, he believed their patron saint S George was noted for chivalry. As an old inhabitant of the borough, it gave him great pleasure to be there, and thus to witness the flourishing state of Parkstone. He believed that the more Parkstone was known throughout the length and breadth of the land, the better it would be for the place and the more prosperous it would become.'

The vote was passed by acclamation, and the Mayor replied on behalf of the Mayoress, saying:

'That, in thanking the company on behalf of the Mayoress for the cordial manner in which they had accepted the resolution, nothing could have given Mrs Cocker greater pleasure than to open these, the first municipal buildings in Parkstone. Those buildings had not been erected before they were wanted, as the residents had desired them for many years, and now he hoped the place would be benefited by them. It would be gratifying to them to know that the Council had seen their way clear to grant the use of the room in which they were assembled as a public reading room, and that it would become a branch of the Poole Public Free Library. Therefore ladies and gentlemen and the working classes generally would have the free use of that reading room. He was glad to say that they had a sufficient sum in hand, after paying for the erection of that building, to enable them to well furnish that room. The builder had spent less money than the Surveyor's first estimate of the cost. Mr Cross had carried out the work in a most excellent manner, and he was afraid that he had rather under estimated the cost, but he (the Mayor) should be exceedingly sorry if that proved to be the case and Mr Cross was in any way the loser. These were magnificent buildings, and would stand, so to speak, almost for ever. During the progress of the building it was satisfactory to know that not a single accident or misfortune had occurred to any of the workmen engaged thereon. Referring to the remarks of Alderman Farmer, the Mayor said he claimed to be a Parkstone man, but at the same time he was a borough man and not a sectionist. The erection of that building ought to conduce to the prosperity of Parkstone. In times gone by Parkstone was considered a village. Fifteen or twenty years ago no doubt that was true. Ten years ago it must have been a considerable village, but now they had municipal buildings in the place it was a village no longer. He believed that it would tend to bring Parkstone into greater prominence, and add to its prosperity. The Mayor concluded by proposing a vote of thanks to the Borough Surveyor and contractor for the efficient manner in which they had carried out their duties in connection with the erection of that building.'

The ceremony finished and the National Anthem performed by the band, the company was hospitably *entertained by the Mayoress at tea in the marquee, while music was performed in the large room by a string quartette.*

The children of the elementary Schools of the Parish were given tea in S.Peter's Schoolrooms at the cost of the Mayor. Some 650 children in all were entertained, grace being said by the Rev C M Gane. After tea Mr Leonard Browne and the Vicar expressed the thanks of the children to the Mayor, who said how pleased he and the Mayoress had been to entertain them. After this the children raised long-continued cheers for the Mayor and Mayoress, and the Sports in the Three Acres Park, commenced before tea, the band assisting."

The Family Links

The fire station had double doors facing on to the cross roads, and there were two police cottages close by in Salterns Road. Denis **Gooding** recalls that in the 1930's the Volunteer Force had a Dennis fire engine, and at one time the officer in charge was Joe **Lee**, followed later by Jimmy **Osmund**. As the fire engine emerged through the double doors, whoever was at home in one of the police cottages would jump on to the rear of the fire engine; Denis **Gooding** remembers one name, that of Constable **Habgood**.

The following are relevant entries in the 1918 Kelly's Directory:-

Britannia Road - East Side

Poole Public Free Library (branch reading room) <u>Mrs Moore</u>, caretaker.
Salterns Road - West Side
Borough of Poole Fire Brigade (Parkstone Fire Station) (Capt. W. Winton, chief officer; James Hardy foreman fireman)

Alma Cottages

1 Oates, Tom
2 Loader, John
3 Elton, Reginald
4 <u>Moore, Ernest</u>

The family history of a branch of the Dean family tells us that when Rose Ann **Moore** died on 9th December, 1906, aged 58, she was living with her husband Mark *'above the fire station and library near Ashley Cross in Parkstone'*, and that she was buried in Parkstone Cemetery. Mark **Moore** remarried in 1909, to Emma Amelia **Joyce** 1866-1932 at Parkstone Wesleyan Church (Methodist) in Salterns Road on the corner with Wessex Road. She was known to the children as Aunt Kate.

A relative visited Uncle Mark Moore and Aunt Kate *'above the stables in Lower Parkstone'*, and Mark and Kate moved into 4 Alma Cottages, the first house in Salterns Road beyond the former mess room. The cottages were demolished in 1991 and replaced by two houses, also called Alma Cottages. Another relative remembers passing the cottage when Mark was very ill *'the road surface was covered in straw to deaden the sound of horses hooves'*.

In 1995 the first house in Salterns road is number 2, occupied by Mr and Mrs Alf **Christopher**. Facing on to Salterns Road, their house is part of the former mess room and foreman's office and also has right of way at the back of the property on to Britannia Road across the old cobbled stable yard.

The branch reading room, opened in 1900, was the forerunner of today's Parkstone Library. £17.00 was provided for bookshelves in 1927 when the reading room was adapted as a part-time lending library; and in 1934 Poole Borough Council gave the library the use of the fire station after the opening of the new one in Wimborne Road.

1994

Until 1994, two steps had to be negotiated to enter the library, the counters were in part of the old council offices and the bulk of the shelves were in that part of the building which once housed the fire engine. A complete refurbishment took place in that year, a new layout designed and computerisation took place.

The entrance was re-aligned, to do away with the two steps, and direct access is now possible to the left - when the work was carried out it was found that an entrance had previously been in that spot. The children's section has been considerably enlarged and separated from the main area; and the new counters, specifically built for the computers, are now where the children's corner stood.

Computerisation has taken the place of the manual system and gives staff faster access to relevant information such as numbers of books out on loan and titles which have been reserved. The majority of shelving is still in the space where the fire engine was kept, and there is room for 10,000 books.

V

The Motor Trade

i *Parkstone Motor Company*

Homelake House, in Station Road overlooking Parkstone Park, stands on the site occupied by Parkstone Motor Company from 1930 until 1985.

The business started in 1900 as the Parkstone Motor and Cycle Company (PMC) by a Mr **Hine**. The premises (now part of Viney's) were in Parr Street and two brothers, Major D F and Captain A A **Ward** were the directors.

Mr Leslie G **Adams** joined the company in 1928, from Walters Garage where he had been an apprentice, and stayed with PMC right through until after 1985 when the business moved to Cabot Lane, acting as consultant to the new owners. He died in 1991, aged 86.

Joining Parkstone Motor and Cycle Company as a salesman, he eventually became a junior director when Mr **Hine** retired; and in due time Captain **Ward** resigned leaving his brother, Major **Ward**, and Mr **Adams** as directors.

The War Years

At the outbreak of the Second World War in 1939, Major **Ward** and most of the senior staff left, being reservists. Mr Leslie **Adams** continued running the business as managing director, except for a period of war service with the Ministry of Supply. Exempted from active service on health grounds, Mr **Adams** formed and ran the local Home Guard mobile section, stationed at Parkstone Motor Company.

The war years saw the organisation appointed area petrol station for the public, also serving the Army, ARP (cleansing station) services and BOAC (British Overseas Airways Corporation). It was appointed official tyre depot for the area, repairer under GRO and Ministry of Supply, car hirer to Army camps and RAF stations. After the war it returned to normal trade and included a self-drive hire department.

In 1945-6 Mr Leslie **Adams** and Major **Ward** (now Colonel) were joined on the directorate by Mr I F **Ward**, Colonel **Ward** eventually resigning, leaving Mr **Adams** and Mr **Ward**. In the early 1950's Mr **Ward** emigrated to Canada and Mr Leslie **Adams** continued in full charge of the business, being joined by his son, Mr Donald **Adams**, in 1962. In 1968 he obtained the MG franchise and in 1969 Mr B **Hilton-Foster** joined as a director.

Motoring Memories

Pat **Varallo** was on the staff at Parkstone Motor Company from 1931 to 1978 and will be remembered by many Parkstone people. She died in 1986 and Leslie **Adams** described her as *'a most loyal and hard working, and liked member of PMC'*. After her retirement Pat **Varallo** wrote down some of her memories and these give us an interesting and descriptive insight into what was once an important part of life in Ashley Cross. Her words are used here with the permission of her sister-in-law, Mrs M **Varallo**. The *'Haynes'* referred to must surely have been the chemist, whose shop was on the corner of Station and Approach Roads where is now Isabel's Restaurant.

Written by Pat **Varallo** -

'Over the years at PMC as recorded by a mere office wallah from June 1931 to October 1978.

June 1931 - premises consisted of Garage faced by two showrooms with offices at rear. Workshop, underground stores, forecourt and five hand operated petrol pumps.

Directorate - L G Adams and D F Ward.

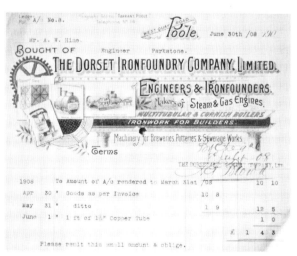

An old invoice addressed to Mr A W Hine of Parkstone Motor & Cycle Company. The hole in the middle indicates that the invoices were kept on a spike.
Courtesy: Donald Adams

Office Staff - Misses W L Fry (Senior), K Stockley and P Varallo.

Salesman - Mr R Morgan.

Petrol Station and Wash Bay - Mr Brumwell replaced by Mr J Isaacs.

Workshop - J Evans (Foreman), Mechanics - L Stevens, F Brown, C Hembury, Apprentices - E Evans, J Blackwell, R Warboys.

Apprentices Stores - J Pike, A Chisman, Electricians - A Jupe and R Lawrence, Grease Bay - F Teague.

Working hours - 8am-1pm / 2-5.30pm Sats 8-1pm - 47½ hour week.

Wage rates - Foreman fixed rate £3.10.0d. per week. Mechanics 1s.3d. per hour. Electrician 2s.0d. per hour. Office - top rate £2.0.0d. per week, assistant £1.10.0d. per 40¼ hour week.

Sample charges - Petrol - No.1.Nat.Benzole, Pratts and Shell 1s.2d. per gallon. B P Commercial 11d. gallon. wax and Simoniz polish 4s.6d. Garage - 1s.0d. per night. Grease and oil 7s.6d. A straightforward decoke was done within one day's working hours at approximately £2.0.0. plus gaskets including collection and delivery.

Staff changes up to 1939 were few - the odd apprentice came and the senior one was elevated to higher grade. Miss Stockley left in 1932 and Miss Fry in 1935 to get married leaving me with new juniors Miss Wilcox and Miss Mizen. Business moved along slowly but surely - new cars were sold at average price £300 to £650 plus number plates and delivery charges.

Dealerships were for Morris, Hillman and Wolseley and popular buys were Hillman Minx and Wolseley Hornet. Warranty Claims were unknown - complaints few and far between.

So the years progressed - customers were spoon fed - various the jobs from cashing cheques, giving loans, minding children, looking after dogs, storing goods and various typing jobs (on one occasion actually typing a book for a budding author living in Alton Road - chapters supplied weekly). Of all trades, Garages seem to collect the most hangars on - folk with nothing to do and all day to do it in migrated to our office, especially around morning coffee or tea time - coupled with the odd insurance bod and car salesmen. The cold weather always drew them in to stand with their rears warming around the fire - on one occasion a hire purchase rep singed the back of his overcoat and trousers - terrible smell of singeing wool in the office.

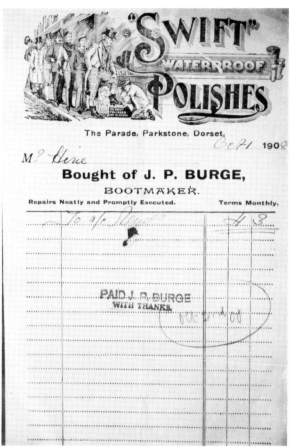

Invoice dated 1st October 1908 addressed to Mr Hine of Parkstone Motor & Cycle Company.
The Parade was the row of shops between Parkstone School and Central Hotel.
Courtesy: Donald Adams

Pat Varallo who worked for many years at Parkstone Motor Company.
Courtesy: Mrs M Varallo

Apart from normal trade there were other events to brighten the year - preparation of Vincent Budge's S.S.I. for Monte Carlo Rally - he being partnered by L.G.A. - it was a more personal Rally than those organised today, sponsored by Manufacturers.

October saw the local Parkstone Players Amateur Operatic production at the Rollerdrome - L.G.A. was Secretary/Treasurer and PMC was suitable venue for seat booking, hence we became booking clerks, crossing off seating plan according to tickets sold.

November brought Armistice Day and Major Ward insisted that we sell poppies - even supplementing payment from petty cash.

Office clothing - dark, long sleeved dresses (some difference today!!), special permission had to be obtained one hot summer (1934) to be permitted to wear short sleeves.

Other Memoirs - Having to go on the carpet and explain to Major Ward why I spent 2d. out of petty cash to buy a pencil - we never had new office equipment - secondhand where necessary - old wind up clocks from Trents scrap cars.

Joan Fry and I having to confess that we had allowed Jack Blackwell to have credit for cigarettes - after reprimanding us, his good conduct money was stopped for a month, whereupon his father came in and wanted to know the reason why we were having to deduct 1s0d. per week from his weekly wage of 7s.6d.

That hot July day when J Isaacs and Blackwell were washing J Haynes car - Blackwell found a bottle in the boot and had a good swig - a quarter of an hour later the imbiber was flat on his back writhing in pain - against his will we shoved a glass of very salt water down his throat and made him violently sick - (Old man Haynes had been out shooting with his pal Bonnett - goodness knows what was in that bottle) anyway we cured him.

Worker's Priority Travel Credential issued to Pat Varallo for use on the buses during Second World War.
Courtesy: Mrs M Varallo

As there was no convenient place for the local ambulance, it was garaged at PMC, Mr E Paddock (of fish fame) drove it. A telephone call came through on the special phone provided - there had been an explosion at Holton Heath - Col. Ward took the ambulance himself collecting Mr Paddock on way, but they were not required as most of the casualties were dead - quite a lot of local people bereaved.

Another auspicious occasion was when Corner Garage at New Road, Ferndown was acquired - (by this time office had been moved into ground floor of Westhill, house next door) - Mr Ronald Adams was managing it and brought in accounts and cash weekly for attention. Being mostly a cash trade and with a hand written till, discrepancies arose - unknown to the hierachy we made illicit trips to Ferndown to make corrections and agree takings before ruling off. We hated DFW being rude to RA - this saved the sparks from flying.

DFW's bi-annual continental holidays were always welcomed when peace and quiet reigned in the office. In spite of our ups and downs we were happy and enjoyed our work.'

War Memories

With Joan Fry going - Joan Wilcox, Gwen Mizen and I strove to carry on until 1939 when "call ups" were in the offing. Joan and Gwen were eventually called up, leaving me to carry on.

No doubt with his military mind DFW foresaw the war years ahead and got some of our men to join his Territorial Unit and others of age he signed up with the Reserves - consequently when that black day arrived in September 1939 all the men had received calling up papers - departing and leaving just LGA to carry on the business with a 17 year old improver, two apprentices and some odd job bods.

The local authorities immediately commandeered an odd petrol pump from which A.R.P. officials were to be served - that was the start of things. Then there was a hue and cry for all cars to have "blacked out" headlamps - having mostly all the local doctors on our books we scoured the district for cake baking tins which were converted for such use until official covers were manufactured. Working hours went by the board, we stayed until such jobs were completed.

Petrol was rationed - continued selling and ordering on coupons received, until such time as instructions were received that all petrol tanks had to be emptied and filled with water as a precaution against invasion - fortunately LGA was wise enough to delay this transaction, whereupon we were designated as Official Petrol Station - it would have caused a furore - petrol and water don't mix!!

A mobile Home Guard section was formed - Mr Adams being in charge - this was based at PMC - my office was used for meetings etc. Much later the sergeant in charge called to say they were a box of live grenades short - these were found in the cupboard they'd installed - I should not have sat so quietly there had I known - I was eventually given the wooden box in which they had been packed and which, up to the time I left PMC, was used as a container for wage packets. The actual garage was requisitioned, firstly by the Army, the Navy and eventually the RAF. All three Services did duty there, but what I failed to see as they just hung about the place, I could have given them plenty of jobs.

The fall of Dunkirk brought Col. Budge and his Grenadier Guards unit with a plea that LGA find them some transport - calls went out to all local garages and customers with laid up vehicles and they were on the road again. This was the start of car hire for Services - we supplied civilian cars throughout war years to Bulford Camp and RAF at Middle Wallop, Tangmere etc. Our Workshop was used for essential road users ie Doctors, Nurses etc and we were authorised Ministry of Supply repairers.

What a headache rationing was. We had ample stock of 'Pool' spirit as it was called but could not supply without coupons. BOAC flying boats were coming into Poole Harbour then and we supplied all their cars which greatly helped towards sales. What a 'to do' at the end of the month when all relevant coupons had to be submitted - queue forming all round Park - waiting to be served and at 2s.1^1/2d. per gallon the set price. We all "mucked in" at serving - my first tip - 9d. change encouraged me to get a Red Cross box as a means of helping, as by this time we had learned that F Brown, F Teague, R Warboys and G Medley were P.o.W.'s (Prisoners of War). The box soon got full and I was so pleased but it didn't last long - somebody decided they needed the money more and rifled the box. Never found out who, but had a good idea.

By this time Mr Adams had been transferred to R.P. Unit at West Howe and whilst doing a job there he was able to keep oversight of garage which was a great help to me.

At onset of war I promised Col. Ward that I would not volunteer but await call-up - this I did but after reporting was told to carry on with what I was doing

Parkstone Motor Company, Station Road. September 1984 before demolition.

until I heard further - this was it. Civilians certainly did their bit.'

Post War Memories

'Eventually hostilities ceased and we were back to square one. Things were not easy - so many goods were in short supply - for every car sold we had to supply six covenant forms duly completed. The men were coming back to their old jobs - so nice to see them again - Sonny Brown was the only one not to return.

Col. Ward came back but the war had taken its toll - he suffered blackouts in the office which we were dared to report, eventually he left to reside on a farm in Devon, Ivor his son became Director with Mr Adams and life moved on quietly. Eventually Mr I Ward emigrated to Canada.

By this time we had acquired Austin Dealership and did justice to it, it was definitely a sellers' market - the Post War salesman "never had it so good". Petrol was rationed for some time which resulted in LGA acquiring Door to Door Hire Service - staff used as spare time drivers - we had various contracts for this service, the catering manager for Queen Mary and Queen Elizabeth used us for leave, and H.M. Tax Collector for visiting outlying districts etc - interesting jobs for drivers.

When petrol rationing was abolished this service petered out and PMC Self Drive was formed - new cars being obtained for this purpose - contracts from various Assam tea plantations for staff furloughs, likewise Iran and Iraq petroleum companies. Various staff dealt with this, eventually A Rendell who was suitably geared for this job took over until the time of his retirement, when the increased purchase price of vehicles made it prohibitive.

Mr I Davies became Works Manager followed eventually by Mr Fay. Mr E C Barker took over office *management and was eventually replaced by Mr R Starkey who remained until his retirement, and so PMC flourished.*

Donald Adams, Leslie Adams' son, became a Director and took over Car Sales having trained with Austin Distributors.

The Directorate was joined by Mr Hilton Foster, eventually relieving LGA for semi-retirement. Premises were altered and enlarged - "Laurel Bank" previously purchased for office space was bulldozed and the ground used for car parking, as was the shop adjoining in Station Road.'

Pat **Varallo's** memories ended here with this last paragraph -

'All this and more - but my days at PMC came to retirement in 1973 - plus a further five years doing the odd two days a week, saving me from becoming a complete cabbage. Time takes its toll - just memories are left.'

Among the Dealerships in the 1970's and 80's were Peugeot, and VW and Audi - in 1982 they won the Dealer of the Year Award. When the site in Station Road was sold in 1985 to McCarthy and Stone, PMC was bought by Wycombe Marsh Garages and relocated to Cabot Lane, near Creekmoor; later being renamed Diamond Cars.

Pat **Varallo** mentioned Mike **Fay**, who was with Parkstone Motor Company for 29 years. Coming from a village near Tisbury in north Dorset, he remembers looking for a job after completing his National Service, and took out a newspaper advertisement. PMC replied and he joined them in October 1957 first as an improver/mechanic, then

Parkstone Motor Company - an Allegro promotion evening.
From left: Mayor of Poole, Leslie G Adams and Donald Adams
Courtesy: Donald Adams

works manager, service manager and eventually took over as general manager in 1984, one year before the site was sold. He was made redundant in 1986, and is now service manager for the Derek Warwick garage, opposite Parkstone Post Office.

One or two other names may jog people's memories - John **Herriman**, Jim **Arnold**, David **Tremain**, Douglas **Pike** and Arthur **Witts**.

David **Tremain** remembers his apprenticeship days - John **Herriman** was his tutor and during the winter they serviced the milking equipment at George **Jennings** farm, next to his South Western Pottery. At the age of 16, David **Tremain** was very impatient to start driving and when John **Herriman** left him sitting at the farm in the large 6-8 seater jalopy used as transport, he grabbed the opportunity and took the wheel. *'The car had a centre throttle and in no time at all I had landed the vehicle in the ditch against a tree. As can be imagined, my face was scarlet, especially as a tractor was needed to get the car back on the road!'*

ⅱ *Westminster Garage (Parkstone) Ltd*

There is no mention of a garage in Commercial Road in the 1918 Kelly's Directory, 1939 quotes Brixey and Butler motor garage, and the entry in 1961 lists Westminster Garage (Parkstone) Limited motor agents, 137 Commercial Road Tel: Parkstone 284. The site was once occupied by offices of the NatWest Bank.

It is believed that during the Second World War the garage was used for a section of Army Transport. It was later owned by the Aireton family, market gardeners, and in 1962 Mr Peter **Barnes** bought the business from a Mr **Newbold**.

*There were still two petrol pumps on the pavement when I took over in 1962,' Mr **Barnes** said, 'but soon afterwards these were inspected and the tanks found to be leaking. My licence to sell petrol was revoked, mainly I suspect because the authorities wanted to stop petrol being sold on the pavement.'*

The premises had a workshop and all the requisite lifting gear, and in a store upstairs Peter **Barnes** found an Aladdin's cave of brand new interesting 1920's car accessories, such as cigar lighters. The main side of the business was selling cars and in this he was ably assisted by the then 19 year old Frank **Spriggs**. *'I became aware of his potential selling abilities and offered him a job and Frank stayed with me for ten years until I sold the business.'*

The Ronnie Biggs Tale

An incident in the mid-1960's added a certain amount of excitement to a wet Saturday afternoon for Peter **Barnes** and Frank **Spriggs**. A fellow, recently returned from Australia, came into the showrooms wanting to buy a second-hand car for cash, and chose a Rover 2000 for around £1500. The deal was done, cash handed over and the car driven off by its new owner. Peter **Barnes** then went up the road to get an Evening Echo, on the front page of which was a picture of Ronnie **Biggs** (of the Great Train Robbery) together with the information that he had just returned from Australia with lots of cash.

Returning to the garage he said to Frank **Spriggs**, *'we have just had Ronnie Biggs in here paying cash for that car, and there is a reward for information about him'*. Frank then read the rest of the words in the Echo and replied, *'you can have my share of the reward'*. It seems there was a quote saying that anyone "shopping" Ronnie Biggs would get their kneecaps broken by his pals!

As Peter **Barnes** set off home round the park he saw a policeman and wound down his window to ask *'would you like Ronnie Biggs?'* The policeman shot off to his nearest telephone box and before long the address (Wallisdown Way) given by the cash buyer was surrounded. The new owner of the Rover had not yet returned but his mother invited the policemen inside where, on the mantelpiece, they saw a photograph of her son/Ronnie **Biggs**. On his eventual arrival home, the poor fellow was immediately pounced upon by the hordes of detectives, only to find that he was a *'look alike'* Ronnie **Biggs** who happened to have recently returned from Australia and who wished to pay cash for a car! Incidentally, he was a Parkstone Traffic Warden.

Peter **Barnes** also owned Bolloms the cleaners and the shoe repair shop at 133A. When the National Westminster and National Provincial banks along that stretch of Commercial road merged, he approached them with the thought that they would not wish to continue operating two separate banks so close to one another. So it was that the whole site was redeveloped, probably around 1975, and Peter **Barnes** went into business elsewhere.

Frank **Spriggs** can now be found, with his son Howard, running his own business, Valley Motors in Branksome.

▦ *The History of Derek Warwick (Bournemouth) Ltd*

The entry in the 1918 Kelly's Directory for Bournemouth Road states Frederick Walters and Co. garage, in 1939 Walters and Co. (Parkstone) Ltd. motor engineers, and 1961 Walters and Co. (Parkstone) Ltd. Exide Battery Service Station and Motor Engineers Tel: Parkstone 705, 706, 707; and many people remember Peter

Walters as the proprietor. It is now Derek Warwick (Bournemouth) Ltd.

In June 1948 a Poole Industrial Products Exhibition was held in Poole Park and in the programme (price 6d) the following editorial appeared:

'Walters & Co. (Parkstone) Ltd., Parkstone Hall Garage, Parkstone. Tel: 705 & 706. 'We are exhibiting an Engraving Machine of unusual construction, giving a large working table with attachments for handling work where accuracy is essential. During the war period it proved invaluable, working in connection with almost every trade.

'This is a small section only of the business trading as Walters & Co. (Parkstone) Ltd. which was commenced in 1913 by Fred Walters as Motor Agent, later appointed one of the original Exide Battery Service Agents. Other sections of the business include a Wireless Repair Department, which has overhauled 20,000 sets in the past 10 years for our trade friends from all sides.'

The site opposite the Post Office is quite extensive and was once divided into three units with separate operators - petrol forecourt, showroom, and workshop at the back. Recent history of the garage indicates that after the Walters family, a Mr J A **Coupland** ran a 24-hour Breakdown Recovery Service from there, and called it Castle Hill Garage. Johnny **Coupland** sold it to Elfords Engineering (Tuckton) in November 1987, when petrol was still being sold from the pumps, and it was run as a non-franchise garage up to 1990.

The first new car franchise was Alfa Romeo, which lasted for two years until 1992 and then changed to Daihatsu. July 1994 saw the business sold to Derek **Warwick**, former Grand Prix racing driver, who also has the Honda franchise in Southampton and in Jersey, where he lives.

Derek **Warwick's** Grand Prix career ran from 1981 to 1993 when he competed in 147 races. He was British Formula 3 Champion in 1978, won the 2nd World Sports Car Championship, with a Jaguar, in 1986 and again in 1991, was World Sports Car Champion and won Le Mans in 1992; and in 1995 was driving with Alfa Romeo in the British Touring Car Championship.

Robin **Williams** is general manager at the Parkstone garage and the Services Manager is a local lad, Mike **Fay** (see Parkstone Motor Co.) Early in 1995 the selling of petrol ceased and the showroom was revamped, and another franchise, that of the Spanish Seat, added.

The garage now sells used cars and has the dual franchise of Daihatsu and Seat with a fully stocked parts department for both; and a workshop and MOT centre at the rear of the site.

VI

Parkstone Telephone Exchange

Parkstone telephone exchange was opened in 1896 by the National Telephone Co. Ltd; and the following entry appeared in The National Telephone Journal of November 1907:-

'Dorsetshire Poole and Weymouth Exchanges existed in 1892, and Parkstone and Dorchester were opened in 1896. The next exchange to be established was Bridport, in 1899, followed by Portland in 1900, Sherborne in 1903, Wimborne and Swanage in 1905, Broadstone, Wareham and Preston (near Weymouth) in 1906, and Upwey in 1907; a total of thirteen in all.'

According to the National Telephone Company's list of sites and buildings dated 1908, the exchange was situated in Church Street (Parr Street), with a lease of six years from 1906, and the annual rent was £30.0.0d.

The first telephone directory was issued in July 1896 with these entries -

1	CARR, Gibbs & Son	Wine Merchants	Station Road
4	CARTER, William		Kinson Pottery, Parkstone
4a	CARTER, William		Private Residence
2	STAFFORD & Co. Ltd.	Prov.Merchants	Station Road
3	STAFFORD & Co.Ltd.	Prov.Merchants	Ashley Road Upper Parkstone

In the 1897 directory George **Jennings** - Terra Cotta & Brick Works at South Western Potteries appeared; a year later the Retreat Hotel (R W **Cornutt**) in Upper Parkstone and Branksome Railway Hotel (Albert **James**) were on the telephone. The number of telephone subscribers had risen to twelve in 1899 and included **Taylor** Bros Butchers, Game Dealers in Commercial Road, and **Wood**, J S Veterinary Surgeon at Walton Lodge.

The architect of the original Parkstone School (later Parkstone Grammar/Ashley Cross Girls School), Walter **Andrew** appeared in the 1900 directory, as did **Ingram** T K Nurseryman, Seedsman, Florist at Parkstone Nurseries, **Lush**, G J (forerunner of Viney's) Corn, Seed Merchant at

Salisbury House and **Walton**, Mark proprietor of the Sloop Hotel (now the Conjuror's Half Crown).

Three Public Call Offices were shown in the 1902 directory at Guest Buildings (Parr Street), one in Bristol House (J Allen & Co) Station Road and another in Upper Parkstone; and the number of subscribers had risen to 36 to include the Headmistress at Sandecotes School, **Bonnett** J Provision, Fish Merchant in Commercial Road, **Haynes**, J A Chemist, **Watkins**, H G Clergyman at Lilliput House and **Van Raalte**, Charles on Brownsea Island.

The 1904 directory had 58 entries for Parkstone, with the addition of **Bingham & Hall** Ironmongers, Engineers, Plumbers in Commercial Road, **Downland**, S T Innkeeper Britannia Inn, **Frampton**, S J W Butcher in Commercial Road, **Kilford** & Co Confectioners, Bakers, Caterers in Salterns Road and Commercial Road, **Leverett & Frye**, grocers in Station Road, **Miell**, C E Hotelkeeper Beehive Hotel, The Poole District Electric Traction Co Ltd and three numbers for the Police - stations at Branksome and Beeches Villas, Bourne Valley and the Police Sergeant at Montrose.

Telephone Tales

Kelly's Directory of 1918 indicates that a Telephone Call Office was to be found in Parr Street (Guest Buildings) between **Wilson's** the builders and Joseph **Wilcox** hairdresser. Mrs Gwen **Pritchard**, who worked there as a telephonist for a few years, remembers a tiny room housing the equipment and five young ladies working in cramped conditions; there was a coal fire and only just enough space to turn around in their seats. Gwen **Pritchard**, now aged 85, was brought up in Branksome and came to live in Parkstone over 50 years ago after her marriage. Her father, Arthur **Parker**, was a Deputy Church Warden at St Peter's Church and Gwen herself was the last child to be baptised there by Canon **Dugmore**.

Increasing Technology

By 31st March 1922 Parkstone was a magneto hand restoring indicators exchange, with 239 exchange lines and 265 telephone sets connected; and between 1st April and 30th September 1927 became a central battery No 1 exchange when there were 914 exchange lines and 1056 telephone sets.

Parkstone Post Office was once in Station Road (now Wessex Needlecraft) and moved to the purpose built premises in Bournemouth Road in 1935; at the same time the parade of shops were erected on the site where once stood four houses - Oak Lodge, Springfield Lodge, The Lodge and Woodside. The telephone exchange then occupied rooms above the new Post Office and later moved across the road, probably in the 1950's.

A paragraph in The Post Office Gazette indicates that *'at 1.15pm on Wednesday 28th June 1972, Parkstone CBI exchange was replaced by a Crossbar (TXK1) satellite exchange with STD and will retain the name Parkstone. All numbers will change and will be within the range 740000 - 748999.'* At that time subscribers could directly dial the Speaking Clock, 999 Emergency Services, and Subscriber Trunk Dialling facilities were introduced. By then there were 8249 exchange lines with 11463 telephone sets connected. International Subscriber Trunk Dialling came between 1st April 1974 and 31st March 1975, and there were 8267 exchange lines with 11741 telephone sets.

In December 1990, to celebrate the transfer of Parkstone to the digital telephone network, Poole's Mayor Cllr Mrs Ann **Stribley** called the Mayor of Parkston City in South Dakota. This small American town was the only place to be found in the world with the same name as Parkstone.

On 14th and 15th May 1994 the Parkstone exchange was open to visitors, who were able to see the £1.4 million System X digital exchange and distribution frame which was installed in 1990 and copes with 250,000 calls a day whilst taking up only a tenth of the space needed by its mechanical predecessor. The system can take 28,000 calls at the same time and is the busiest exchange in the south of England for residential calls.

Guided tours enabled people to go 12 feet down underneath Bournemouth Road to inspect the fibre optic and regular cables in the 90 yard long tunnel, which until the recent end of the Cold War doubled as a fall-out shelter. Visitors were also able to see the engine room with a stand-by diesel generator for use in the event of a power failure. This is powerful enough to light a town the size of Ringwood or to drive a cross-Channel ferry - it is tested regularly but rarely used - the last time was February 1992.

A mobile exchange, Castle Hill, was opened between 1st April 1969 and 31st March 1970 as an Automatic Non Director strowger exchange. There were 158 exchange lines with 180 telephone sets, and these had increased by March 1975 to 2475 exchange lines with 2740 telephone sets connected.

The Post Office Gazette dated 21st May 1975 quoted the end of the Castle Hill mobile. *'At 1.15pm on Wednesday 28th May 1975 Castle Hill customers in the ranges 2000-2999, 3000-3999, and 4100-4499 will be transferred to Parkstone TXK1 and their numbers will be changed to Parkstone 6-digit numbers to become part of the Bournemouth LNS.'*

My thanks to BT Archives for historical information, 2-4 Temple Avenue, London EC4Y 0HL.

A Strowger telephone as used in automation experiments at Epsom, Surrey

Almon B Strowger (1839 - 1902) worked as an undertaker in Kansas City, and discovered that his local telephone operator was related to a business rival and diverting some of his calls. He decided to design an automatic system to prevent this from happening in the future. The first British version was opened in 1912 and remained in use until digital switching took over in the 1980s.

VII

St John Ambulance Brigade

The Poole Corps of the St John Ambulance Brigade began life in St Peter's Church Hall in the 1920's and several Ashley Cross traders voluntarily gave their time to serving the organisation. Stanley **Viney** (Viney's Garden Centre) and Ernest **Paddock** (Mesher and Paddock, fish shop) manned the ambulance which was parked at the rear of the fish shop which once stood at the cross roads; and Denis **Gooding**, who went to St Peter's School and took a considerable part in the civic life of Poole, remembers his years as a Cadet under Stanley **Viney**. At one time, there was a First Aid hut on Parkstone Green (where the toilets now stand) and this contained a wheeled cart carrying a stretcher.

The St John Ambulance Brigade, the leading First Aid training organisation in he UK, had its early beginnings in the Crusades in the Holy Land and started nationally in earnest in 1887, and the Mottoes of the Order are *'Pro Fide' For the Faith* and *'Pro Utilate Hominum' For the Service of Mankind.* The skills and training are kept up to date ranging from simple First Aid to Defibrillation techniques and Trauma management, Emergency Aid and Public First Aid Training to Industrial Training Courses. The Poole Division, with its headquarters at 4 St Peter's Road had, in 1995, 50 Badgers (6-10 year olds), 60 Cadets and 70 Adult Members.

The Official Opening and Blessing of these headquarters took place on Sunday 21st July 1950 and a printed programme (price 1s.0d.) set out *The Romance of a Movement',* as follows.

Thirty years ago, in the Parish of St. Peter, Parkstone, the present Poole Corps was born; one Ambulance Division (Parkstone) under the Divisional Superintendentship of Mr E L Scott, and one Nursing Division (Parkstone) under the Divisional Superintendentship of Mrs Scott. They met in the Parish Hall. Mr A J Cuff (afterwards Corps Superintendent of Bournemouth and later County Officer of Hampshire) was the first Ambulance Officer. Both Divisions were formally registered in 1921, the Ambulance Division just one month too late to claim

the distinction of being the first of its kind in Dorset, the Nursing Division claiming that honour.

In 1928, Mr E Paddock replaced Mr Scott as Divisional Superintendent, and in 1929 a new Ambulance Division (Poole) was formed, Mr E Bennett, a local Chemist, being its first Divisional Superintendent, and Dr E S Bowes (from Totnes) its Divisional Surgeon. Meanwhile on the nursing side several changes of Officers had taken place; Mrs Scott being succeeded by Miss De La Combe, to be followed later by Mrs Swayne, Miss E M Sharp, Miss Lever and Mrs K Martyn. A second Nursing Division (Poole) had also come into being under the Divisional Superintendentship of Mrs G Candy.

During this period the men moved house many times, leaving the Parish Hall for the Parkstone Liberal Club and thence to the Weymouth Road Drill Hall, until both men and women found a common meeting place once more in Wessex Road, Parkstone, at the rear of the Old Post Office. In 1929, the necessity for the formation of a mixed Corps arose, the total number of men and women being then 89. This was accordingly formed with Mr E Bennett as the first Ambulance Corps Superintendent and Mrs Boyle as the first Nursing Corps Superintendent. Mr S Brackstone succeeded Mr Bennett as Divisional Superintendent of the Poole Ambulance Division and Mr J M O'Hara replaced Mr Bennett and in 1939 was succeeded by Mr E Paddock. In the same year Mrs K Martyn succeeded Mrs Boyle. These war years carried with them heavy responsibilities. In 1943 the mixed Corps were divided into two Corps, an Ambulance Corps, (male) and a Nursing Corps (female). In 1945, both Mr Paddock and Mrs Martyn received County rank and were succeeded respectively by Mr F C Bryant and Miss C M Timbury, the present Corps Superintendents.

In 1948 a crisis arose, and both Corps faced together the problem either of finding suitable premises in which to train, or of going out of existence. They took temporary refuge at 'Brackendene', 2 Commercial Road, Parkstone, and finally acquired 'Melville', 4 St Peter's Road, Parkstone, near the little Parish Hall which had seen their birth.

The building is a gift to the order of St John of Jerusalem from all the men and women, boys and girls, both past and present, of the St John Ambulance Brigade (Poole Corps) and also from their many friends. The spacious Lecture Hall at the rear is the gift of Mrs Ruth Fairholme, a Canadian citizen, in memory of her Aunt, the late Miss Minnie Hewett, for many years a resident of this ancient Borough of Poole.'

The events for the Official Opening ran from 4.45pm onwards -

1. **Arrival** of the Countess of Mountbatten of Burma (Superintendent-in-Chief) accompanied by His Worship The Mayor and the Mayoress of Poole (Alderman and Mrs Ross MacMahon), Major Wheatley, MP, Robed Knights of the Hospital of the Most Venerable Order of St John of Jerusalem and Presidents and Officers of the St John Council and County of Dorset.

2. **Welcome** by the Corps Superintendents (Mr F C Bryant, Miss C M Timbury.)

3. **Presentation** of Distinguished Guests: Corps Nursing Officer Miss M E Le Blanc SRN, (Ashford, Kent, formally of the Poole Corps). Mrs Clara Atkins. Mr F C Bryant.

4. **Presentation** of the House key on velvet cushion (handworked by Mrs Sandford of Weymouth) by **An Ambulance Cadet.**

5. **Opening** of Door by the Countess Mountbatten of Burma.

6. **Blessing** of the House and Lecture Hall by the Reverend E C Harris, Rector of Poole and Chaplain to His Worship The Mayor, assisted by the Rev H J Coulson, Vicar of St Peter's, Parkstone.

7. **Presentation** of the Title Deeds of the Property to the Knights of the Order of St John by the Corps Superintendents (Mr F C Bryant, Miss C M Timbury).

8. **Signing** of the Visitor's Book and Inspection of the House and Lecture Hall by the Countess of Mountbatten of Burma and her party.

9. **Arrival** of the Official Party in the Marquee adjoining 'Melville' (erected by kind permission of

H M Ministry of Works) and Presentation of a Bouquet (the gift of Miss Rowell) by Mrs E Cobb, Senior Member of the Poole Corps.

10. **Tea** in the Marquee.

This official programme for that day in July 1950 was very informative, and also set out a brief history of the property calling it 'The Story of a Home':-

*'On the 19th Day of October, 1878, Sir Ivor Bertie Guest of Canford Manor in the County of Dorset, Baronet, demised unto one Daniel Hitching, of Bournemouth in the County of Hants, "**All that piece or parcel of land situate lying and being in the Tything of Parkstone, in the Parish of Canford Magna, in the said County of Dorset, containing in the whole 53 perches or thereabouts**"; in consideration of the expense which he the said Daniel Hitching "**hath been at, in building and completely finishing one substantial messuage or dwellinghouse with outbuildings thereto**". In consideration of the premised the said Daniel **Hitching** on his part covenanted that he would not use the said premises thereby demised for the purpose of a shop, alehouse or other place for carrying on the trade or business of a tavern keeper, alehouse keeper, or retailer of beer or any other liquor, tallow melter, soap maker, brewer, distiller, butcher, slaughterman, farrier, founder or smith, or any other noisome or offensive trade business or occupation and would not make, or suffer to be made any bricks upon the said land.*

On the first day of June, 1880 the ownership of the property passed to one Robert Walter Swinburne, of Parkstone aforesaid, Esquire, whose widow on the fourth day of April 1887 conveyed the same to the Reverend Edward Clayton, Clerk in Holy Orders, and Honorary Canon of Chester.

On the first day of May, 1894, the Reverend Canon Clayton conveyed the same to the Reverend James Walter Gregory, clerk in Holy Orders, and for many years Curate serving the Parish Church of St Peter, Parkstone, who remained there until his death on the 1st July, 1932. His widow, the late Mrs Octavia Gregory, remained during her lifetime in the property, which after her death was ultimately acquired by the Venerable Order of St John of Jerusalem (namely in 1949) as a Headquarters for the St John Ambulance Brigade (Poole Corps).'

Melville, 4 St Peter's Road is still the Headquarters of the Poole Corps of the St John Ambulance Brigade and, apart from the various courses available, weekly meetings are held on Tuesday evenings.

VIII

Guides and Scouts

i *Guides*  **THE GUIDE ASSOCIATION**

At Parkstone Grammar School a Girl Guide Company (thought to be the 5th Parkstone) was formed in 1918 by Miss **Briant**, a Mathematics teacher. Such was the demand that this later had to be divided into two separate companies. Meetings continued without interruption during and after the Second World War (1939-1945), camps were accepted as part of their routine and from time to time many girls attended international camps. Instead of the regulation light blue scarves, the girls wore their school ties.

Sadly, the company had to be disbanded in 1967 when the age of entry to the Guides was dropped to ten years and girls entering the school were already settled in other companies. Many old girls recollect Miss M **Barnes** as Captain and Miss Enid **Cowles** as her Lieutenant. It is believed that there was also a Ranger Unit.

7th Parkstone - Congregational Church (now United Reformed) - was formed in 1921 with Miss **Potter** as Captain and Mrs **Potter** as Lieutenant, and up to 1947 the following people were involved as Leaders: Miss E **McKay**, Miss M **Tawney**, Miss N **Bradshaw**, Miss E **Compton**, Miss M **Haines**, Mrs **Crowhurst**, Mrs D E **Crew**. Mrs Alice **Suckling** was Captain in 1949 with Miss Barbara **Pollard** (now **Dutfield**) as her Lieutenant, and those that followed were Mrs Beryl **Titman**, Mrs L **Haig**, Miss Maureen **Bessant**, Miss Kathleen **Buck**, Mrs A M **Savin**, Mrs Mavis **Pearce** and Mrs Fay **Johnson**.

A Brownie Pack certainly existed for many years and Miss Vivienne **Batterson** (her parents were Scout/Cub Leaders) was Brown Owl at one stage. The 7th Parkstone disbanded around 1988.

6th Parkstone - St Peter's Church - is part of Parkstone West District in the Poole East Division. The Company was first registered on 20th May 1921 and it is thought that a Brownie Pack came into existence in 1923. The first Guide Captain was Miss E **Pontifex** with Miss **Kentish** as Lieutenant, and through to 1944 the names of Guide Leaders

included Miss M **Guppy**, Miss M **Holmes**, Miss E M **Marshall**, Miss D **Marston**, Miss V **Grant**, Miss D S **Lowry-Curry**, Miss P **Stonehouse** and Mrs J **Samson**. The Company then appeared to have disbanded for a short while, as it was re-registered in 1949 with Mrs **Stokes** as Captain. Miss F **Roots**, Miss A **Julyan**, Miss Nesta **Rees**, Mrs Madeleine **Jones**, Miss Jennifer **Peckham**, Miss Barbara **Graves** and Mrs M **Dilmas** were involved as Leaders through till 1963 when, again it seems, the Company was disbanded.

Mrs Barbara **Handscombe** re-started 6th Parkstone early in 1972 (registered on 9th May), assisted by Mrs Marie **Parkins**; the demand was such that a second Company was formed. Run by Mrs Pat **Sheppard**, it had to be disbanded five years later because of lack of Leaders.

There is now (1995) one Guide company, two Brownie Packs and one Rainbow Unit. The Guide Company is run by Mrs Marie **Parkins** and Mrs Shirley **Pedrick**, with four young helpers/Assistant Guiders - Emma **Cockwell**, Claire **McClumpha**, Heather **Parkins** and Claire **Stock**.

The District Commissioner was Miss **Barnes** when the St Peter's Guides were re-started in 1972; and one of Mrs Barbara **Handscombe's** memories of her years as a Guide Captain is a very proud one. The Guides had attended a Thinking Day Service at Westminster Abbey, and on her return home Mrs **Handscombe** received a telephone call from Guide Headquarters to say that 6th Parkstone had been voted the *'smartest company in the Abbey that Day'*. The Bournemouth Echo picked up the story and a piece appeared in the paper a few days later.

The log book of 6th Parktone St Peter's from September 1980 to the summer of 1995 makes interesting reading. Amongst the general Guiding activities at the end of the year was *'a visit to a church arranged by Skip (Freddie Bunceball)'*, then on Christmas Eve Skip died and the church was packed for his funeral service. On 8th February 1981 his Thanksgiving Service was held; his splendid camp fire blanket can be seen on display inside St Peter's Church.

'Atrocious weather, high winds and snow' gave the Guides a chilly week-end at Dudsbury, the Guide Camp Site near

Parley Cross, on 24th April. Lynda **Holloway** received her Queen's Guide Award at the Saturday evening camp fire from Mrs Helen **Rench** and Mrs Barbara **Handscombe**. Later in the year, overnight hikes were undertaken in July and a week-end camp at a Scout hut in Langton Matravers. A charity walk for Stoke Mandeville raised £79.00.

The Guides manned the Hot Dog stall at the Regency Fayre on Parkstone Green (Park) on 18th June 1983, and attended the Festival of Youth later that year. On 14th February 1984 three girls received their Queen's Guide Award - Carol **Gatward**, Rebecca **Shering**, Lizzie **McArthur**.

8th June 1984 was *'Dorset Day'*. A giant Jamboree was held at Baiter to celebrate the 75th anniversary of the founding of the Girl Guides; guest of honour was Lady Patience **Baden-Powell**, Chief Commissioner since 1979 and grand daughter-in-law of the Founder, and a pageant portrayed major landmarks over the last 75 years.

In 1993 some of the Guides attended Woodlarks - A Special Camp; this report was written by Rebecca and Ruth **Stockwell**:-

'Woodlarks is a camp for people with physical and mental disabilities. Every year Guides and Rangers from Bournemouth come to Woodlarks for their Guide camp. The girls that are able to, sleep in a tent, but the others sleep in a dormitory. Everyday the girls go swimming in the morning or afternoon. When not swimming they do other activities such as craft, drama, music. We also had campfires and a cook-out. On the last day there was a big party with the theme of America.

'Every girl has a helper, but the helpers usually have at least two girls to look after. They help with everything the girls do and get them up in the mornings.

'Woodlarks is really good fun and we enjoyed it a lot. The only bad thing is getting up at 6.45 each morning!'

1995 was described as a very busy year with maximum numbers; and a most enjoyable summer camp was held at Bucknowle, near Corfe Castle at the beginning of August.

There are two Brownie Packs at St Peter's - 6th Parkstone and 12th Parkstone, the latter is run by Helen **Maidment** and Pat **Radcliffe** and the 6th Parkstone by Rachael **Shering** née Thompson and Lynette **Hilton**. When Rachael herself joined the Brownies in 1970, Mrs Margaret **Woodford**, who is now President of Parkstone West District, was Brown Owl. As a Guide Rachael was chosen by Councillor Mrs Doris **Webster** to be the Mayor's Guide 1979/80; and remembers attending the Civic Service at St

James' Church, the Beating of the Bounds ceremony and a Civic Ball. Going on to obtain her Queen's Guide Award, Rachael gradually progressed from helping with the Brownies to becoming Brown Owl, the Brownie Guider.

Rainbows are the youngest unit within the Guides and were introduced a few years ago. Mrs Angela **Storrey** neé Stacey and Mrs Janet **Ashman** look after those at St Peter's.

ii Scouts

The 2nd Parkstone Scout Troop was in existence from June 1910 to 1937. It was started by the headmaster of Parkstone School (later Parkstone Grammar), Reverend Stanley E **Moss**, soon after the school opened and disbanded when he retired and the school became an all girls establishment.

A few years ago a man walked into Baden-Powell House in London and handed over the Troop scarf and flag belonging to 2nd Parkstone, together with a log book. The man in question is a descendant of Reverend Stanley E **Moss** and these historical items are now in the possession of the Borough of Poole Scout Council.

There was an uninvited guest at the wedding of Lieutenant General Sir Robert S S **Baden-Powell** KCB, KCVO to Miss Olave **St Clair Soames** at St Peter's Church on 30th October 1912 at 12.45pm. A 13 year old Scout with the 2nd Parkstone, Eric **Seaward**, was a server at the church and had attended the customary mid-day Holy Communion Service. Knowing there was to be a wedding immediately afterwards he decided to stay and watch, not knowing the tremendous impact the bride and groom would have on future generations of young people.

5th Parkstone Cub Pack - Congregational Church (later United Reformed) - during the time that Mrs **Batterson** was Akela of the Cub Pack, she had the assistance of Jack **Stocker**. When Mrs **Batterson** eventually retired, he took over as Akela and Gordon **Langley** became Baloo and his wife, Barbara, an Instructor. Towards the end of the 1960's (probably 1967) the Cub Pack amalgamated with Lilliput Sea Scouts, and the two Packs were called Port and Starboard. This was due to the fact that the Scout Association did not then allow a Cub Pack to run unless there was also a Scout Troop; and the one at the Congregational Church had disbanded.

The Port Pack, run by Gordon and Barbara **Langley**, wore red/gold scarves and met at the old chapel in Lilliput Road (opposite Holy Angels Church) before making their home down at Turks Lane. The Starboard Pack, still under the care of Jack **Stocker**, continued to meet at the Congregational Church hall.

Barbara **Langley** recalls that her Warrant was presented to her by the then District Commissioner, Bob **Seward**; and that the activities in Poole Park to celebrate the Jubilee of the Cubs included the making of Go-Karts. Each Christmas there was a joint Candlelight Carol Service with the Guides and Brownies, and it is whispered that one or two daredevil Cubs tries to set fire to the long hair of some of the Brownies!

'In those days of full attendance at meetings and events' Barbara commented *' we had very very long waiting lists, and one GSL (Group Scout Leader) is remembered for putting his son's name on the list just two days after his birth'.*

Although there are no Cubs at the United Reformed Church now, the Lilliput Packs are thriving.

Parkstone St Peter's - this Scout Troop was originally called 6th Parkstone (St Peter's) but the change of title took place on 13th March 1968. The original date of Registration (no 1168) was 26th October 1928 with Norah **Williams** as both Group Scout Master and Cub Master, and Annie **Thomas** and Kathleen **Webster** as Assistant Cub Masters. The address of the Group Headquarters was given as Boys' Institute, Chapel Road and was Controlled (Sponsored) by Reverend Eric S **Tarrant**.

A log book for 6th Parkstone (St Peter's) Wolf Cubs 1934-1946 may stir a few memories - on 25th May 1934 seven Cubs *'go up'* to Scouts, one of these was a Second, Fred **Buncehall**. There was a picnic on 16th June in the *'Scouts Field'* with 1st Lilliput, and for the St Peter's Remembrance Day Parade on 11th November there was a full attendance - Scouts, Cubs, Rangers, Guides and Brownies - and the Two Minutes Silence was held in the churchyard.

In 1935 the St George's Day Parade was held at St Luke's and the Mayor's Drumhead Service in Poole Park on Sunday 5th May. *'Ambulance kept busy owing to great heat'.* 9th June - Miss **Williams**, District Cubmaster, was presented with a framed photograph of the Chief Scout at the County Rally. This is the District Scouts' County Award for Scouters who have done particularly helpful work in the Districts and for the County. The presentation was made by Sir James **Brookes**, District Commissioner.

On 2nd November of the same year a Rally in the Congregational Hall celebrated 21 years of the Wolf Cubs - Sir James **Brookes** KCB, District Commissioner for East Dorset, Captain H C **Mayor** OBE RN, County Commissioner for Dorset, and Mr H **Colquhoun**, Commissioner for Wolf Cubs, were present.

An entry for September 1936 tells us that when meetings resumed after the summer break, Dennis **Ricketts** was in the Isolation Hospital with Typhoid fever (this was the serious outbreak in Poole and Bournemouth which resulted in 51 deaths). He was still in hospital on 17th October but 10th November saw his return to the Pack.

There were changes in Leadership in 1937. *'Miss Cull (Baloo) had to leave and Miss Rabetts took her place. Mr Caswell (Kaa) one of 'our' Rover Crew, having just won his 'Golden Cords', has joined us - he was one of the Pack's first Cubs at the time of its formation in 1928.'*

Then in December 1938 the pack said *'Farewell to Akela'* who had been with the Pack for seven years, first as Bagheera and then as Akela for twelve months. Miss **Godfrey** and her sister have already agreed to stand in and, with the help of Miss **Williams** will maintain the high standard which Mrs **Millard** has obtained. A Camp Fire was enjoyed and Akela was presented with a bronze statuette of a Cub doing the Grand Howl.

War Years

The Second World War broke out on 3rd September 1939, and this is the entry for September - *'We meet the first problems caused by the war. Owing to the black-out (and later to air raids) meetings could not, except on light evenings, be held at night. In addition local children would attend school one week in the mornings and evacuee children in the afternoons. This arrangement changed over every week. Meetings, therefore, had to be held every other week. November - school was now held all day and the Headmaster agreed to Cubs leaving at 3.30 to attend meetings which were fixed at 3.30 to 5.00pm. This was later reduced to 4.30 so that the Cubs could reach home before black-out'.*

In July 1940 The Shack at the Britannia Hotel was lost, owing to a change of ownership; and problems continued with air raids becoming more frequent. For security reasons, County and other badges bearing the name of the town, had to be removed from uniforms; colours too were removed.

The Founder of the Boy Scouts, Lord **Baden-Powell**, died on 8th January 1941 and a Memorial Service was held in St Peter's Church on the 19th, which only Sixers could attend owing to the large number of Scouts, Guides and others being present.

November presented Leadership problems, Akela (Miss **Godfrey**) and Chil into the WRNS and WAAF; Rama and Baldo (Ken **Moggs** and F **Buncehall**) to other work.

In February 1942 the 6th Parkstone became guests of 5th Parkstone and met on alternate Saturday afternoons in the Congregational Hall (Akela Miss **Boley**). Church Parades were still held at St Peter's and so tradition was kept alive. Then in the March Miss **Boley** was called to the Colours and 5th and 6th Parkstone Packs segregated again, the 6th to meet in the Parish Hall on Wednesday evenings; and for the first time Cubs were allowed to join in the March Past at the annual St George's Day Parade.

Entry for July - *'quite fortuitously Akela and Chil were on leave at the same time and visited the Pack to a great welcome. They went to church and every Cub was present on Parade! Mrs Robinson was Warranted as Akela.'*

The death, on Active Service, of a former Cub was announced in 1943. Sergeant James E **Jeffery** had been a Flight Engineer in the RAF, and lost his life in a Stirling bomber which ditched in the Channel; the plane had run out of fuel after a bombing raid. Later in the year, when the Cubs gave a party in the church hall, a collection was taken and sent to the B-P Memorial Fund in memory of Sergeant **Jeffery**.

A report in the St Peter's Church magazine for August 1946 states that Scouts and Guides met in Poole Park to greet the new County Commissioner, Sir Thomas **Salt**; and a County Rally at Dorchester in June was the first since the war. 400 were present from all over the county. St Peter's Pack were second out of 66 entries and they were awarded a Red County Ribbon for the totem and the Tydeman Cup to be held for one year. They received congratulations from the Poole Association.

From the Log

A log book for Parkstone St Peter's Scouts 1929 to 1945 is unusual in that it is not very informative about the Troop's activities and mainly contains mentions of Courts of Honour; nevertheless a few entries are of interest. During 1932 there was a week-end camp at Wool in June, the summer camp was held at Leonard's Farm, Beaulieu and the Troop helped at a fête at the Rollerdrome (this was either the site opposite Parkstone Post Office or in Church Road where the Christian Scientist Church is now). Tickets for a Troop dance in October were single 1s6d (7$\frac{1}{2}$p), double 2s6d (12$\frac{1}{2}$p), Scouts in uniform 6d (2 $\frac{1}{2}$ p) Scouts not in uniform 9d (4p).

In 1933 note was made that all Scouts who were late or failed to attend Church Parades were called before the Court of Honour to give their reasons; and in December 1934 *'it was decided that this year toys will not be repaired as the Christmas Good Turn'.*

28 Scouts and four recruits were recorded in June 1936 and it was decided to organise the Troop into four patrols - Hawks, PL (Patrol Leader) **Caswell**; Wood Pigeons, PL **Bodger**; Eagles, PL **Murray** and Peacocks, PL **Broadhurst** - eight Scouts to each Patrol including PL's.

1937 was the Coronation Year of King George VI and Queen Elizabeth (the present Queen Mother), and a party from the Troop took part in the torchlight procession and two volunteers (!) sold programmes. On Saturday, 5th August of that same year, ten Scouts were on duty at Compton Acres. (It is not known what form their duties took).

January 1938 - the Troop was granted the use of the Britannia Hotel Hut in Britannia Road as a new headquarters by Mr **Bushell**; it was called *The Shack'*. The name of Fred **Buncehall** appears as a Rover Scout in October 1939.

No mention is made of any difficulties during the years of the Second World War (1939-1945) but on 23rd July 1944 there was a Memorial Service at St James' Church for Lord **Somers**.

The *'Festival of Britain'* (1951) is mentioned in a 1950's log book. 1953 saw the Coronation of Queen Elizabeth II (our present Queen) and one Scouter and nine Patrol Leaders attended a National Scout and Guide Coronation Service at Westminster Abbey; the Scouter was F C **Buncehall** and one of the Patrol Leaders was William **Murray**. A pantomime was staged each year; and among the 29 1st Class Scouts representing Dorset at the Jubilee Jamboree at Sutton Coldfield was Anthony **Littlewood**.

The Present Day

In 1995 there are two Beaver Colonies, two Cub Packs, one Scout Troop and one Venture unit. The joint Group Scout Leaders are Nick and Sharon **Wilkinson**, Scout Leader is Joe **Askell**, the Cubs are run by Marian **Lohez** and Penny **Watkins**, and the Venture Scout Leader is Mark **Collins**.

The royal blue scarf worn by Parkstone St Peter's is distinctive (if not unique) in having an emblem of crossed keys. This is a memorial to a teenager who died in a motor cycle accident in the early 1990's; he was not a scout but his parents, who are members of St Peter's Church, wanted a positive sign to indicate the strength and vigour of the St Peter's youth organisations.

A fund raising activity in April 1994 by the 12-strong St Peter's Groups will no doubt be entered into the current log book as having been a successful event. A mile of coins, neatly laid out across Parkstone Park (the Green), raised £1000 towards the cost of replacing their 'Y' registered minibus. Adult Group members and supporters stood beside the busy Commercial Road and at Ashley Cross junction with collection buckets and the Beavers, Cubs and Scouts placed the coins in a neat double row winding around the footpaths of Parkstone Park. *'Following last year's (1994) fatal minibus crash on the M6 which involved a Ford Transit, our own vehicle, which also has side facing seats, was immediately taken out of service within the Group'* explained the Fundraising Chairman, *'and we aim to raise £7000 in order to purchase a vehicle with front facing seats and safety belts. This mile of coins means that we are half-way to reaching our target; and a variety of further fund raising events are planned, including a Gang Show'.*

St Peter's Church was full to overflowing on Sunday 23rd April 1995 when Poole East District of the Borough of Poole Scout Council held their annual St George's Day Parade. Curate at St Peter's, Reverend Richard **Davey**, took the service and Father Stephen **Lake** (Vicar at St Aldhelm's) Borough Chaplain, gave the address entitled *'St George and the Dragon'.* The Deputy Mayor of Poole, Councillor F **Winwood**, and the Mayoress Mrs **Winwood**, attended the Service together with the MP for Poole, Mr John **Ward** and Mrs **Ward**. Afterwards the Parade marched along Commercial Road and into Park Road, where the Deputy Mayor took the Salute, and the Parade was then dismissed in Poole Park.

My particular thanks to Alex Wilson of the Poole Scout Council for his assistance with this chapter.

For further information see 'The Story of Scouting' at the Waterfront Museum, Poole Quay; and the Denis Gooding Centre, Layton Road, Upper Parkstone - Headquarters of Poole Scout Council.

8th June 1984 - 'Dorset Day Jamboree' in Poole Park to celebrate the 75th anniversary of the founding of the Girl Guides.
Courtesy: Mrs Marie Parkins

Cadman's the Bakers - 1936 Harvest Festival.
Mrs Kath Raymond is to the right in the window. The three young lads are her brothers John, Charles and Andrew.
Courtesy: the late Mrs Kath Raymond

2nd Parkstone (Lady Baden-Powell's Own) - Founded 1911 at Parkstone School (later Parkstone Grammar/Ashley Cross Girls School). Closed 1937.
'Visit to Southampton Docks - 1932 camp'
Courtesy: Alex Wilson

Cadman's the Bakers now Bennett's the Bakers, Britannia Road.
Courtesy: the late Mrs Kath Raymond

Family Businesses

i Bennett's the Bakers/Cadman's

Bennett's the Bakers in Britannia Road is well known to most Ashley Cross and Parkstone residents for the Bennett family have been there since 1949. Prior to that time, it was called Cadman's (E E **Cadman**) and was certainly trading in 1918 (Kelly's Directory) and possibly for several years before the First World War (1914-1918).

Anthony (Tony) **Bennett** is a Cornishman and when he left school in the early 1950's his parents, Claude and Winifred, bought Cadman's and so set the scene for a family tradition covering several decades. Together with his wife, Margaret, Tony **Bennett**, who trained at the South Devon Bakery school and in Southampton, took over the running of the business in 1964; and their three children Suzanne, David and Mark have all become involved with the bakery. Both sons have won numerous awards within the bakery trade, and Mark's 100 Gold Medals include two from Hotel Olympia, the country's foremost catering exhibition. His most recent accolade is the Pierre Scacco Award, which gives him a week in the Richemont School in Switzerland, the world's finest confectionery centre. The Award, through the Worshipful Company of Bakers, is in recognition of all his past achievements.

1986 was a proud year for Bennett's the Bakers for they had the honour of providing a wedding cake for the marriage of Prince Andrew to Sarah Ferguson. Work on the cake, which stood over 6' tall and had four tiers, was shared between the family - David was in charge of the actual mixture, Mark carried out the design and decoration and father kept an extremely close eye on the whole procedure. Transporting the cake up to Buckingham Palace in their own van was a nerve-racking experience; and a replica was on display in their Britannia Road window.

In recent years the old bakery at the rear of the shop in Britannia Road has been completely rebuilt and up-to-date equipment installed; and the number of retail outlets have increased from five in 1986 to 12 in 1995.

Ellen Elizabeth **Cadman** ran the bakery in days gone by; it is known that she married Fred **Teague** and lived on Brownsea Island where he was a pottery worker. He died at an early age, possibly from influenza, and Ellen Elizabeth married again, to a Londoner, George **Cadman**. The bakery had two horses and they used to deliver bread to Sandbanks over the sandhills to the Coastguard station.

Information about 'Granny Cadman' was passed to me by one of her descendants - Mrs Kath **Raymond** (Ethel Louise Kathleen née **Rigler**) aged 90, who has her own memories of the bakers.

'Grandad Cadman used to have a pony and trap to take people to Sandbanks. Poor Gran worked very hard to bring up her family, taking in washing, doing the choir surplices for St Peter's Church and serving in the small shop which sold ice-cream, sweets, bread, flour, yeast. We used to drive (pony and trap) to Bovington Camp with bread for the army in the 1914-1918 war. I went with Grandad, who was very small with a long white beard. He and Gran Cadman were very happy. Gran lived to 86 years old; she was beautiful with blue eyes and golden hair which she plaited and kept long even when it was white, a woman who worked hard and had a wonderful sense of humour.

Uncle George worked for a Mr Lush who owned a corn merchant shop in Parkstone (Vineys), also a high wheel gig and a beautiful prancing horse in which he took his lady love; this was quite an event.

Uncle George delivered coal and trusses of hay and straw, also pea and bean sticks. He also looked after the two horses. George used to come up to the bakery and cut the chaff on the chaff cutter Gran had. I used to help by tying a rope round my waist and going backwards and forward as the wheel and knives cut up the hay and straw for the two horses.

Gran had a cockatoo which was white with a yellow top knot and we taught him to talk and say "good night George". He used to dance the sailor's hornpipe which he copied from me; I was only 12 years old then. He would perch on my shoulder and share a cup of tea and then screech and screech.

Gran Cadman was a wonderful character, everybody loved her. She would look across the yard by the bakehouse towards Poole Park and say "Ah, 'tis dark down there at Pugs Hole. We be in for a storm". I never really ever quite knew where Pugs Hole was and as Grandad Cadman was a Londoner and Gran Cadman from Dorset, my brothers and I used to find the conversation quite hilarious at times, especially if Gran tried to talk posh. I remember once two ladies came to see the bakehouse and remarked how clean everything was so Gran said "Oh yes, we even whitewash the coke", which we all took turns in carrying in buckets each day to burn in the furnace to bake the bread and cakes etc.

Easter was hard work with 4000 and more hot cross buns which were made, cooked and delivered, leaving the shop at 4 o'clock in the morning. When you came back you slopped out as we called it. No rest, but they

Family Businesses - Viney's. 'A Chamber of Trade Outing in 1928 - outside Viney's Farm, Blakedene'
Courtesy: Mrs Doreen Viney

Family Businesses - Viney's.
Bonnett's Stores - now Viney's Garden Centre'
Courtesy: Mrs Doreen Viney

were delicious and would keep for weeks. We were worn out and very tired but happy.

We were not rich, just able to keep out of debt and hope for better times. As I think back on those days of candles, hot bricks to warm the beds wrapped in flannel, scorched oil lamps, coal fires, coppers to boil clothes and cook Christmas puddings, fetching shavings from Poole to heat the copper and fetching bracken from the woods nearby for the horses beds, beef dripping, toasting kippers and herrings on a brick by the coal fire, I thank God I had such wonderful parents and a Gran and Grandad'.

I am grateful to Mrs Kath **Raymond** for these descriptive memories, which will surely serve to remind us of the changes which have occurred during the 20th Century. There is still a family connection between Cadman's and Bennett's for Mrs **Raymond's** daughter works on a part-time basis in one of the shops.

Whereas in Grandma Cadman's day around 4000 hot cross buns were made, Bennett's prepare 10,000 on Maundy Thursday, the same number on Good Friday and 5000 on Easter Saturday.

With seven grandchildren, Margaret and Tony **Bennett** can perhaps look forward to the prospect of the family business continuing well into the 21st Century

Mrs Kath Raymond died in November 1995.

⚏ *Viny's Garden Centre*

W ith a pedestrian entrance on Commercial Road, close to the traffic lights, Viney's Limited, Garden Sundries and Nurserymen, can truly claim to be a part of Ashley Cross. Three generations have been involved so far and the fourth (Carolyn, Susan, Sharon and James) already take their share of the work.

Kelly's Directory of 1918 lists George William **Lush**, corn and coal merchants on the south side of Commercial Road, where the public car park is to be found. In the 1920's the shop was sold to farmer John **Viney**, from Blake Hill Farm in Lilliput, grandfather of the present owners Malcolm and Tony **Viney**.

John **Viney**, who had a milk round based at the Blake Hill Farm, carried on trading in Commercial Road as a corn and coal merchant, and when he died in 1932 his wife, Emma and their three sons, Eric, Raymond and Stanley, continued to run the business. In due time, after the deaths of his two brothers, Stanley **Viney** took over as sole proprietor.

Mrs Doreen **Viney**, who is now in her early 80's, came to the area from Stockbridge in Hampshire as a governess to a family living in Parkstone, and eventually became acquainted with Stanley. Their marriage at the Church of the Transfiguration in 1934 was conducted by Reverend **Boyes** with Mr Ernest **Paddock** as best man; and their reception was held at the Bournemouth Pavilion. They had a two day honeymoon in Weymouth before returning home in time to do the stocktaking in the shop.

Mrs **Viney's** memories of Ashley Cross include Police Balls in the 1930's at the Rollerdrome in Church Road (now First Church of Christ, Scientist), Ingram's Nurseries on the other side of the road, Barrett's Stables and Squibbs sweet shop in Parr Street, Flay's the saddlers, Sole the butcher, the double fronted Co-Op shop in Church Road facing the Green, Lannings for curtains, Knights the haberdashers, Cross the builders for coffins and Moorhead fruit and vegetable shop (where Executive Homes is now).

The coal to be sold in Viney's shop came into Parkstone Station on wagons and had to be shovelled off the trucks into sacks early in the morning before the shop opened; and Mrs **Viney** remembers supplying a Christmas tree to Upton House when it was disastrously occupied by Prince Michael of Roumania.

As usual in those days, Mrs Doreen **Viney** was a housewife who stayed at home to bring up the children. But during the Second World War, when most people were either in the fighting forces or in *'Reserved Occupations'*, she turned her hand to helping out in the running of the business.

Stanley **Viney**, who died in 1982, was a well-known figure in the area for many years, being a Special Constable and a Serving Brother in the St John Ambulance Brigade. Together with Mr **Paddock**, he drove the Borough ambulance which was later taken over by the St John Ambulance, whose first headquarters were in Wessex Road. In 1950 they moved to 4 St Peter's Road - it is still the Poole Headquarters as well as an Industrial Training Centre.

Stanley **Viney** attended all sorts of events in Poole in his capacity as an ambulance driver, including the Speedway, and gave 36 years service to the St John Ambulance Brigade. Lady **Wheatley** (wife of Poole MP Sir Mervyn) was a Serving Sister with the organisation, and Mrs Doreen **Viney** remembers travelling to London with her husband and Lady **Wheatley** to attend a St John Ambulance Brigade investiture.

In the early 1960's Viney's was relocated, due to compulsory purchase for a road widening scheme which involved the demolition of all the properties along Commercial Road on the south side from Curzon Road down to the crossroads - 34 J Viney and Sons Ltd Corn Merchants, 30 Quick Cleaners (Raymond Dudley Ltd) Dryers and Cleaners, 28 Mesher & Paddock, fishmongers and poulterers tel: Parkstone 427 - according to the local Kelly's Directory. The properties along that stretch of Commercial Road had long gardens down to Wessex Road, and the space left after the road widening now contains a GP's surgery (Drs **Forbes**, **Whalen** and **Lewis**) and a public car park.

Viney's moved to its present position, into premises formerly occupied by Bonnett's stores, grocers. The site in Parr Street had been used as their store for a number of years and the opportunity was taken of creating the plant centre there, with the car park, and to provide direct access through the shop.

The present proprietors, Malcolm and Tony **Viney**, took over the running of the business when their father semi-retired in the early 1980's; and are constantly making improvements and keeping up with new trends. Apart from their own children, who are all taking their part in the business, long standing members of staff, known to most of the customers, include Ted **King** and Betty **Love**, who have each served the family firm for nearly 30 years, and Andrew **Mills** who joined Viney's as a *'Saturday boy'* several years ago.

It is plain to see that the entrepreneurial spirit inherent in John **Viney** in the 1920's when he added a shop to his farming activities, is still alive and well in the 1990's.

Outside 16 Britannia Road - Gordon Brown, Audrey Thomas, Pat Rigler and Lynne Rigler.
In background the shops and terraced houses demolished for the 1961 road widening.
Courtesy: the late Mrs Kath Raymond.

X

Public Houses and Inns

The five pubs in Ashley Cross have all been in existence for a considerable number of years. The Britannia Inn is mentioned on an 1844 map, a beer house existed on the site of the Central Hotel in 1873, the Bermuda Triangle (previously Bull's Head) was mentioned in the 1918 Kelly's Directory, as was the forerunner of the Bricklayers Arms, and the Parkstone (Station) Hotel was erected as a public house between 1872 and 1876.

In 1995 each one offers a different atmosphere and a variety of attractions. Whilst the Britannia Inn is a family pub with a large television screen predominantly used for sports programmes, the Central Hotel is *the music venue'* for Lower Parkstone, the Bermuda Triangle has a cosmopolitan bar specialising in Real Ales and imported beers, the Bricklayers Arms is small pub patronised by local people and the Parkstone Hotel is a popular venue for Inter-Pub Sports Leagues organised by the licensee.

Britannia Inn

Britannia Inn (Whitbread) 20 Britannia Road. Marked on an 1844 map 'Tything of Great Canford' as premises and garden with John **Eason** as innkeeper. The licensee quoted in the 1918 Kelly's Directory was T J **Hands** and in 1939 it was Frederick **Bushell**. Next door at no 22 was the Britannia Stores - Mrs B **Oram** shopkeeper.

We know that a Mr **Dowland** was licensee in 1900 because, on St George's Day, he complained to the Council that the marquee erected for the opening ceremony of the new Municipal Offices completely blocked the access to his pub. Later, he was given compensation of two guineas by the Council. (*Victorian Poole'* by John **Hillier**).

The licensees in 1995 are Caroline and Simon **Holmes**.

Central Hotel

Central Hotel (Hall and Woodhouse) 81 Commercial Road on the west corner with Parr Street. Deeds in the possession of Hall and Woodhouse at Blandford (Archivist Frank **Pike**) tell us that in 1807

'Hendry Brown Cookman of the Tything in Parkstone in the county of Dorset Blockmaker was the

highest bidder for Lot 11 at public auction at old Antelope Inn in Poole. One acre, one rood and one perch for Lot 11 lying on East Heath in the parish of Great Canford in the county of Dorset bounded on the SE by a road mentioned in Lot 10 in the particular of the said Sale on the south by the turnpike road leading from Poole to Christchurch'.

He paid £23.4.8d.

A Mortgage Deed dated 4th December 1819 from Mr **Cookman** to Thomas **Parr** described Mr **Cookman** as yeoman and Mr **Parr** as gentleman, and the deed was witnessed by H M **Aldridge** and Robert **Davey**, clerks to Mr **Parr** Poole Attorney.

Between 1819 and 1896 the following names appeared in connection with Mortgages, Leases and Conveyances of the property - Mrs Mary **Parr**, Mr Joshua **Gollop**, Rev Isaac **Phoenix** from Marlborough, Robert Henning **Parr**, George **Knight**, John and James **Talbot**, Mrs Sarah Jane **Parr**, Henry Cornelious **Palmer** grocer of Parkstone, James Rickman **Justican**, Edward James **Young**, William George **Barton** of Hereford and Thomas Byard Winter **Sheppard** of Frome.

Records show that *'a dwelling house, grocer's shop and beer house'* existed in 1873 and the premises came into the possession of Hall and Woodhouse in 1896 when Henry **Burden** provision merchant and Leonard Davis **Ballard** coal merchant sold *'the freeholding dwelling, Public House, Grocer's Shop, Cottage, Cellars and Stores, Stable Buildings, garden and premises situate at Ashley Cross to George Edward and Alfred Charles Woodhouse of Ansty in the county of Dorset, Brewers being co-partners in the trade or business of Brewers at Ansty and carrying on the same under the style or form of 'Hall and Woodhouse' for the sum of £3,400.'*

An advertisement in the 1932 Poole Guide describes it as a *'family, commercial and residential hotel with the nearest railway station two minutes away and golf links one mile; the proprietors were Mr and Mrs Harry Howard.'*

The current licensees are Sandra **Trow** and David **Newstead**, who took over on 31st May 1994.

Bermuda Triangle

Bermuda Triangle (previously Bull's Head) Parr Street. The 1918 Kelly's Directory places the property as between St Peter's Elementary Schools and Mrs Sarah **Wicks** shopkeeper, and gives the name of Albert **Seaton** as beer retailer. In 1939 it was described as the Bull's Head at 10 Parr Street with the licensee as Mrs Emily Augusta **Elgar**. It is believed that the landlord in more recent times was Jack **Taylor**, who still lives in Ashley Cross.

The change of name to the Bermuda Triangle came in 1989 when Gisela **Crane** took over. The new interior was created by a film set designer, and what was once a yard and bottle store is now the Boat Bar. Realistic ship's furniture, wooden decks and portholes provide the background for displays of old seafaring gear, charts and press cuttings relating to the, sometimes, unexplained losses in the real Bermuda Triangle in the South Atlantic.

It is believed that the pub once had local connections with Tom Sherrin, a colourful *'larger than life'* character, who was Mayor of Poole in 1964.

Bricklayers Arms

Bricklayers Arms (Eldridge Pope) Parr Street. The archives of Eldridge Pope in Dorchester (Archivist Mr K J **Hutton**) tell us that the first documentation was a Conveyance dated 5th August 1833 of a *'piece of land'* from John and Jane **Hore** with Robert Henning **Parr** to George **Barrett**, who was a bricklayer! And 22nd October 1833 from George **Barrett** to Dianah **Williams** a property *'newly erected'*. It has been suggested that the house may have been built specifically to provide the St Peter's Church masons and labourers with liquid sustenance.

Various Conveyances and Mortgages were transferred, on 27th February 1839, from Dianah **Williams** to Robert Henning **Parr** and thence to H **Mooring Aldridge** (Solicitors), and on 1st July 1872 Alfred Augustus **Allen** to Frederick **Styring** of the Tisbury Brewery *'a beerhouse known as the Bricklayers Arms'*. (Also in that year Frederick **Styring**, a prosperous brewer and owner of public houses in Wiltshire, Hampshire and Dorset, including Poole Brewery, bought the cottage and land on which he later built the Station Hotel). In 1900 Eldridge Pope and Co Ltd acquired both the Bricklayers Arms and the then Station Hotel from Mr **Styring**.

Between 1879 and 1991 the following were tenants at the Bricklayers Arms - Chichester **Mawditt**, A E **Wilson**, Frank Turle **Wilson**, D **Dickenson**, Josiah **Perris**, Mrs Charlotte **Perris**, Arthur John **Renyard** (son-in-law of Mrs **Perris**), J **Rose** (son-in-law of **Renyard**) Mrs **Rose** (the same family ran the pub from 1912 to 1960), W **Turk**, Lionel **Black**, A B **Wark**, and G R **Longcroft** who it is believed now resides in France.

The Bricklayers Arms was under management for a few years from 1991 and during that time loud music caused unwanted disturbance to the neighbouring properties. The pub lost its music licence, and since the arrival of Jan and Harvey **Cowell** in October 1994, the Bricklayers Arms is now a quiet pub with a pleasant garden patronised by local people.

Parkstone Hotel

Parkstone (previously Station) Hotel (Eldridge Pope) 58 Station Road. The earliest deed from the Eldridge Pope archives is dated 1813 - for the sale of a *'piece of land for £5.00'* upon which a cottage was built. The land and cottage were bought by Lieutenant Nathaniel **Brice** RN in 1830, who moved in with his wife Sarah Maria. The Lieutenant, who became a Commander, died around 1864 and on 30th September 1872 his widow sold the land and cottage to Frederick **Styring**.

Sometime between 1872 and 1876 **Styring** built a public house on the land, and as the new adjacent railway station (Parkstone) had just been built in 1874 (Poole and Bournemouth Railway Co), he called his new pub *The Station Hotel'*. The first tenant, from 1876 to 1879, was Eli **Curtis**.

By 1883 the railway was owned by *The London and South Western Railway Company'* and **Styring** was paying them the sum of £1.00 per year for the right of way over the station forecourt; this still happens today, but not at £1.00.

In 1888 the Poole Brewery, which owned all the Styring houses changed the name to *The Parkstone Hotel'* and it was subsequently purchased by Eldridge Pope in 1900 (see Bricklayers Arms).

Past tenants have been Eli **Curtis**, George **Noble**, Richard Alfred **Bennett**, C R **Hayball** (who became a Poole Councillor), Stephen **Short**, George **Hodge**, W H **Willis**, Josiah **Murrin**, A E **Lloyd**, L E **Adams**, H E **Gibbs**, Matilda **Gibbs**, F T **Foddy**, J Cowles, W **Newman**, C G **Cogdale** (during the Second World War Mrs **Cogdale** took over the licence 1941/45 whilst her husband served in the Forces).

Ross **Darby** is the present licensee. A local lad, born in the old Poole Maternity Hospital, Ross is known to many Ashley Cross people and remembers several of the previous licensees at the Bull's Head and Bricklayers Arms.

XI

Personal Reminiscences

i Mrs Marion Lillington

Having lived in Parkstone virtually all her life, the memories of Mrs Marion **Lillington**, who is in her early 80's, give an interesting insight into various aspects of life in this area over the last 70-80 years.

'I was born in Dorchester and came to Parkstone at the age of 15 months. My father Charles Waygood, after 25 years as a regular soldier, was the Sandbanks postman from 1914 to 1937. He was based at the Post Office in Station Road and his 'broken-up' working day was from 5.00am to 9.00pm. On his bicycle he made three daily deliveries in Sandbanks and had to wait two hours before making a collection from the postbox. Taking sandwiches with him he spent those two hours fishing and talking to the Harvey's boatmen, who would supply him with cups of tea. I well remember him coming home one evening and handing my mother the fish he had caught (which was still wriggling) before dashing off up to the Post Office before 9.00pm.'

Mrs **Lillington** went to St Peter's School in Parr Street. The boys and girls and infants were all separate units - Miss **Ward** was headmistress of the girls school, *'Pecker'* **Brookes** headmaster for the boys and Miss **Williams** for the infants - until 1928 when it became a mixed school. Mrs **Lillington** would often stop and watch the horses being shoed at the blacksmiths in Salterns Road on her way to school, but would scamper quickly off when she spied the headmistress walking up the road.

Leaving school at 14 she wanted to work at Poole Pottery and was offered a job there by Mr **Adams**, but her mother would not allow her to accept. It appears that the pottery was then situated in an unwholesome part of Poole with a lot of drunkards hanging around, and her mother had no intention of allowing her daughter to walk those streets.

Marion **Lillington** then went to work at the Reflex Studios in Albert Road, Upper Parkstone where, instead of being involved with the tinting of photographs, she was given the boring task of inspecting negatives. Hating every minute of the work, she stuck it out for six weeks before refusing to stay any longer.

Her next job was with the Model Farm Dairies in Sandbanks Road. Situated opposite Whitecliff Recreation Ground, it was originally known as Harraway's Farm before being taken over after the First World War by Mr A **Munser** and Mr R **Medhurst**. Initially, her job was bookkeeping there but eventually she was in charge of all the stores for the milkmans' rounds.

Marion **Lillington** remembers 1936 very well. *The typhoid epidemic in Bournemouth and Poole in the summer and autumn of that year had extremely serious consequences, with 51 deaths. The Model Farm Dairy was involved and a rumour spread that the infection came from an artesian well on the farm with the suggestion that a cow had fallen into the well and so contaminated the water used for sterilising the milk bottles. But since the diameter of the artesian well was only 4 inches, the story soon lost its credibility.'*

'Eventually the outbreak was traced to a Dorset farm - the farmer's wife had typhoid and their sewage polluted a river from which the cows drank. During other times of the year the milk supplied by the Model Farm Dairy came entirely from their own cows, but in the summer the influx of visitors to Sandbanks meant that we had to buy in "accommodation" milk from other farmers, thus it was that the typhoid reached residents and holidaymakers alike in this area.'

The epidemic bankrupted the owners and the farm/dairy was eventually taken over by Malmesbury and Parsons Dairies, who had a shop in Station Road and later in Commercial Road (where is now the Windsurfing shop).' Marion's husband, Charlie **Lillington** was a milk roundsman for 49 years, starting with the Model Farm Dairies, then with Malmesbury and Parsons Dairies and when he retired it was from Unigate. *'He was devastated when, during the typhoid epidemic, five of the customers on his milk round died.'*

Mr **Lillington's** first experience as a roundsman was before he left school, when he helped to deliver the milk on his bicycle in the Sandecotes Road area at the week-ends.

At the age of 15 (after he left school) he had his own milk round covering Britannia Road, Mentone Road, Salterns Road and part of Sandbanks Road, and up to the beginning of the Second World War in 1939 there were two deliveries per day. Equipped with a 12 gallon brass churn and bucket, a measure with a long handle and half pint and one pint cans on a 'pram' he pushed the milk round the roads and knocked on each door crying *'milko'*. His customers used to take a jug to the front door and he dipped in his bucket for a pint, and there was always *'a drop for the cat'*.

Marion **Lillington** remembers seeing Charlie polishing his churn and bucket in the milk yard at the Model Farm before it was scalded ready for the refill for the second delivery. The milk was not pasteurised in those days, and that second delivery would have been that morning's milking.

It appears that there are still some older folk in Parkstone who remember Charlie as their milk boy, and quite recently someone told Mrs **Lillington** that as a small boy he was always given Charlie as a *'pattern'* in politeness.

Mrs **Lillington's** grandmother lived in Sixpenny Handley, where she was the village midwife and had 12 children of her own. When grandfather died she came down here for a holiday and, at the age of 70, saw sea for the first time - this despite living only 24 miles from the coast. On being taken to the beach and invited to sit on the sands, grandmother declined with the comment *'I am not going to sit on that dirty stuff'*.

Another family memory concerns the wearing of hats; there was a strict dress code in those days with hats being worn whatever the occasion. A favourite outing was to take the open top tram from Poole East (Brown Bottom) to Fishermans Walk, Southbourne. Mrs **Lillington's** mother had bought, from the hat shop in Parr Street, a velvet cloke hat decorated with pansies. On the top of the tram this was caught by the wind and blew off. The tram driver refused to stop for the hat to be retrieved, and Marion **Lillington** remembers her mother, feeling very embarrassed, standing on the pavement in her hobble skirt and white blouse and ***no hat!***

Describing herself as being *'naughty when I was little, wandering off on my own on many occasions'* Mrs **Lillington** remembers the wood where Steepdene is now, the turnip field on which is built Baden-Powell Middle School and the nurseries in Mill Lane. A Mrs **Ricketts**, the midwife, lived in Parr Street. Just past the Bermuda Triangle pub was the Welcome Lodging House and for many years there was a beautiful mimosa tree close to Viney's Garden Centre which only died quite recently. In Commercial Road, near to Epps, there was a brush factory with an archway, and on top of this was a carved head. It is believed that this carving was once in the walled garden at Upton Country

Park and that it is of a Mr **Bennett**, blacksmith. Also remembered is Matchbox Terrace - four cottages opposite the Wesleyan church in Salterns Road, where lived a Miss **Talbot**, Mr **Loader** a postman and Mr **Baker** the chimney sweep.

ⅱ *Mrs Barbara Dutfield*

The memories of Barbara **Dutfield** née **Pollard** are of interest regarding Guides and Ashley Cross in general. She is the daughter of Donald and Dora **Pollard** - her father was a groundsman at Parkstone Golf Club and her mother in service at a house in Bingham Avenue. Her parents, first of all, lived in a terraced cottage in Lilliput Road, now Lagado Close, and then moved to a cottage in Parr Street close to the Bricklayers Arms and Barrett's Riding Stables. The horses in the stables were unhappy during the Second World War air raids and made a lot of noise, and Barbara remembers feeling very scared at the time.

When attending St Peter's School and the air raid siren went, Barbara was able to pop home across the road whilst all the other children had to stay in the school shelters. She remembers the dairy in Parr Street (mentioned by Denis **Gooding**) and particularly the fact of the cardboard tops of the milk which were discs with a hole in the middle - these were very useful for making woolly bobbles!

Barbara was at Parkstone Grammar School 1942-46 and recalls Miss M **Barnes** as Captain of the Girl Guide Company and Miss Enid **Cowles** as Lieutenant; they wore their school ties instead of the regulation light blue Guide scarf. There was also a Ranger Unit at the school. During air raids, instead of being able to go home, Barbara was not impressed by the fact that she now had to stay in the school shelters until the All Clear sounded.

Mrs Alice **Suckling** was Captain of 7th Parkstone Guide Company at the Congregational Church (now United Reformed) and Barbara became her Lieutenant for a few years before moving to 1st Parkstone, whose headquarters were at the Langdon Road Guide Hall (opened in 1931). Barbara remembers that Mrs Mavis **Pearce**, whose husband used to have the furniture restoration business at Park Gates, was involved at one stage with 7th Parkstone Guides.

Reminiscences about her father include the fact that he lost his front teeth at the junction of Lilliput Road and Bingham Avenue - it seems that as a lad he was playing around on his bicycle outside the old police house on the corner and collided with a lamp post! Mr **Pollard** was an Auxiliary Fireman based at Walters Garage (opposite

Parkstone Post Office) during the Second World War, and the shop next door was the Mess. Barbara and the rest of the family used to visit him there during the evenings because he was on call and rarely had an evening at home.

⊞ John E Paddock (Mesher and Paddock)

Mesher and Paddock, fishmongers and poulterers, were originally to be found at 38 Commercial Road, on the south side between Curzon Road and the crossroads where now stands the car park; and in 1955 the shop moved to 28, on the corner of Salterns and Commercial Road. In 1961, when the road widening took place at Ashley Cross, several shops were demolished along that stretch, including the fishmongers.

Initially, Johnny **Mesher** owned the shop and Ernest Herbert **Paddock**, when he came out of the Royal Navy in 1919, worked for him and in due time became a partner in the business. Mr **Mesher** died in 1924 and Ernest **Paddock** then became sole proprietor; he had three sons John Ernest, Ernest Herbert and George Reginald.

Mr John **Paddock**, living in Parkstone, is the son of Ernest Herbert and remembers that the wet fish came into Parkstone Station and had to be collected early in the morning; the fish came mainly from Grimsby with some from Greenslades in Poole. One of his wartime memories is of the tragedy which occurred when a car ran out of control and killed a lady who was queuing outside the fish shop. Long queues for food were part of domestic life during the Second World War, and after that accident police restrictions were placed on the length of queues.

After attending Courthill School, John **Paddock** worked at the Bournemouth Gas and Water Company (now British Gas) before going as boy worker/apprentice at the Holton Heath Cordite Factory, where he remembers, not only the type of work involved but also, the masses of mosquitoes indigenous to that heathland.

A keen Boy Scout with the 7th Parkstone Troop at St Luke's, John **Paddock** gained his King's Scout Award in 1932. 12 years service in the Royal Navy from 1936 to 1948, included six years of the Second World War, following which he then joined his father and brother in the family business.

When the road widening at Ashley Cross took place in 1961 the shop was demolished and John **Paddock** then joined Southernprint (the old Bournemouth Times) and retired in 1982.

He recalls many of the Ashley Cross shops in the 1930's - 'Happy' **Prime**, the grocer (remembered by many others), Alfords the greengrocers, Topps the butcher, Flay's the saddlers, Cross the hairdresser, Mr **Hennings** from the Co-op, who used to call on his mother for her weekly order, Cates in Station Road, Chalkley's Dairy (once John Bates Tyres), and in particular a character called Lucy in Britannia Road who had a mania for not allowing anything to park in front of her property - she used to holler and shout *'don't you park your van there'.*

John **Paddock** remembers the **Battrick** family, as do several other people. When Mrs **Bonham Christie** turned the large **Battrick** family off Brownsea Island, around 1934, they had nowhere to go and eventually found their way to a flat in Commercial Road above Greens, the cake shop. This was 93 Commercial Road on the north side between Parr Street and Bonnett's (now Viney's). There were five daughters and one son, and one of the daughters, Florence, found a job as a cook in Marks and Spencer in Poole High Street and was there for many years, probably up until the early 1970's. She went to live in Britannia Road with her brother, who became a Warden on Brownsea Island after the National Trust took over.

During the Second World War Brownsea Island was a decoy so that the Germans would believe that they had dropped their bombs on Poole; and many people say that the sea between the island and Baiter was black with swimming rats on the morning after the first raid. The rats appeared to have disliked the bombs just as much as the humans!

John **Paddock** still refers to Ashley Cross as *'the village'*; and indeed still meets people who miss the fresh fish which was available at the fishmongers by the crossroads.

Commercial Road before the road widening in 1961.
Demolition of Mesher & Paddock, Fishmongers & Poulterers, 'Families Waited on Daily'.
The Odeon is advertising 'The Greatest Show on Earth'.
Courtesy: Mr J E Paddock.

The Changing Scene

Until 1975, current information about towns in England and their surrounding neighbourhoods was easy to find - all one had to do was look in a Kelly's Directory. Bournemouth, Poole and Christchurch were together in one volume and the information provided was all-embracing, including a street directory, official and public establishments, places of worship, list of private residents, commercial directory and professional and trades directory.

Thus in 1961, we know that Lord **Digby** DSO MC TD was Lord Lieutenant of the county, Captain Richard **Pilkington** MC was MP for Poole; the Mayor was Alderman W H **Cole** JP, Deputy Mayor Alderman A J **Stokes**, Recorder Malcolm **McGougan** MA, Sheriff Councillor E S A **Clapp** and the Councillors for the Parkstone Ward were Mr Leslie G **Adams**, Mr Thomas W **Sherrin** MBE and Mrs W **Udall**.

Published each year, Kelly's Directories first appeared in the early 1800's and ceased publication with the 1975 edition. The 1939 issue listed 40 directories for the London area and 70 for the rest of England, and that for Bournemouth, Poole and Christchurch cost 10s.0d (50p) - with 1,976 pages it was worth every penny.

The following are listings from the street directories of 1918 and 1939 and more or less cover the roads within the conservation area of Ashley Cross. At the end of the chapter, the current shops as in December 1995 are listed.

Approach Road	
from Curzon Rd to Station Rd	
North Side Kelly's 1918-19	**North Side** Kelly's 1939
Clarence Terrace	22 Appleton, Fredk.W.L.
1 Lockyer, Fredk	(Lyndale)
2 Hartness, Mrs	20 Gould, Jack
3 Jupp, William	18 Wheeler, Martin
4 Percy, Henry James	16 Agent, Mrs
	14 Sidney, Edwd.Hy
Glen Terrace	12 James, Fredk
1 Allner, George	10 Spicer, Lot
2 Spicer, Lot	8 Allner, Rt.Friend
3 Allner, Robert	6 Reeves, Geo.S. (Bybank)
4 Reeves, Geo.S.	4 Austin, Benj M.
5 Austin, Benj Montague	2 Field, Geo. Edward
6 Luff, Mrs	
	here is Wessex Road
here is Wessex Rd	

Bournemouth Road	
from Commercial Rd	
South Side Kelly's 1918-19	**South Side** Kelly's 1939
Mew H.G. house furnisher	2 Hibbs, Norman H. F.S.I.
Williams, James cycle agent	auctnr. (AltonChambers)
Parrott, A.J.	2 Coles, J.S. coalmerchant
Aldridge Sidney, watch maker	4 Mew, H.G.horsefurnisher
Cates, Fredk.Jas (Ashover)	6 Whitbread Miss G. baker
Walters, Frederick	8 White, Frank
Walters Fredk & co garage	8 Lloyd W.&Son bakers
Twist, Edward R. (StrettonCt)	10 Avery Mrs Gertrude, florist
	12 Dugdale, Alfd.butcher
	14 Walters, Frederick
	16 Walters & Co (Parkstone)
	Ltd. motor engineers
	16 Centaur Groom (Sales) Ltd
	18 Barker, Frederic M.B.,B.S.
	London, M.R.C.S.,L.R.C.P.
	physician & surgeon (Stretton Ct)
	Tel.No. Parkstone 195

Bournemouth Road	
from Commercial Rd	
North Side Kelly's 1918-19	**North Side** Kelly's 1939
here is Springfield Rd	Post Office Parade
	Midland Bank Ltd. (A.G.Wollen, Man)
Oak Lodge	11 Dash, Samuel R.
Springfield Lodge	11 &12 The Lino King, housefurnisher
The Lodge	10 Grace, Ronald Wm
Woodside	10 Parkstone Same Day Cleaners
	dyers and cleaners
(these presumably were pulled	9 Honess (E.L.Honess, prop)
down and Post Office Parade built)	hairdresser
	Barclays Bank Ltd. (J.E.L.Poulsonman)
	Nicholls Fredk.Wltr.(BankHouse)
	6 Worron, Jas.Wm.tailor
	5 Dunningham, Alt.Georgechemist
	4 Blackmore Percvl.ironmonger
	3 Walker(E.F.)&Whinnerah(E.) statnrs
	2 Lacey, Cyril Jn.tobccnst
	1 Model Farm Dairies (B'th) Ltd
	1 Williams Mrs
	Parkstone Branch Post Office
	then Dorchester School

Britannia Road
from Ashley Cross

West Side Kelly's 1918-19	West Side Kelly's 1939
Ashley Cross Cottages	Ashley Cross Cottages
1 Eyers Geo. Chimney Sweep	2 Norman, Reginald
2 Arnold Frederick	4 Toms Mrs
Wilton Cottages	Wilton Cottages
1 Call Mrs	6 Broadbent Miss
2 Dunford Herbert	8 Dunford Herbt. Geo
Oakfield Cottages	Oakfield Cottages
1 Mitchell Benj boot maker	10 Squire, Albert
2 Robins Albert Edward tailor	12 Barnes, Albert
Cadman George shopkeeper	
Jubilee Cottage	14 Cadman's, bakers
Rigler Mrs (Fern Cottage)	16 Symonds, Cecil R
Britannia Inn Percival T.J. Hands	18 Watson, Geo. Hy
Oakland Cottages	20 Britannia Hotel, Fredk.Bushell
4 Galton John	22 Oram Mrs B. shopkpr (Britannia
5 Lovelace Mrs Emily	Stores)
6 Ayling Alfred	Oakland Cottages
7 Joyce, James	24 Galton John
Emmott Philip Rickman	26 Lovelace Arth.Jn.Jas
M.I.C.E. (Willow Brae)	28 Ayley Mrs
Hammett Mrs (Oakleigh)	30 Joyce, James
Bugg Harry T (Telscombe)	
	32 Tucker Ernest Reginald
	(AshbourneVilla)
	34 McKissack, Rowland (St Agnes)
	36 Noad, Herbt Scotford (Baroda)
	38 Leng, Albt (Goldsborough)
	40 Larkin, Ernest (Hawkwell)
	42 Towner, Ernest Ed (LittleOrchard)
	46 Kent, Gordon Alfd.Douglas
	(WillowBrae)
	46 Discharged Soldiers' Window
	Cleaning Co. (G.A.Kent)
	48 Hammett Miss (Oakleight)
	50 McBridge Maj.Stuart Geo.. O.B.E.,
	M.C. (Telscombe)

Britannia Road
from Ashley Cross

East Side Kelly's 1918-19	East Side Kelly's 1939
Poole Public Free Library (branch	Fire Brigade Station
reading room)(Mrs Moore, caretaker	Poole Public Free Library (branchreading
(AshleyCross))	room) (Ch. Harvey, caretaker)
Poole Borough (depot)	Poole Borough (depot)
Beasley James (Brooklyn)	1 Hambridge Geo.Hy
Oak Cottages	3 Cooper, Merthyr Jas.carsforhire
1 Old Robert	5 Eyers Leslie Arth. birdfancier
2 Hatcher George	7 Hardy, Edw.F.(Conowindra)
Wiltshire Cottages	9 Knight, Fredk.Wm (Bincleaves)
1 Cross, Frank Stanley	Oak Cottages
3 Cross, William James	11 Cross Hy.Jas
	13 Greany Christopher
Tucker Leonard (Dunmore)	Wiltshire Cottages
Grace George (Dunmurry)	15 Cross Frank Stanley
Harris William (Dunmurry)	17 Jones, Dennis B
here is Mentone Rd	Dunmore Cottages
	23 Grace, Geo.
	25 Matthews, Hy. George B.
Viney Mrs (Arfleet)	*here is Mentone Rd*
Pearcy E.P. (Parkside)	
Baker Mrs (Leymore)	27 Viney Mrs (Arfleet)
Wilson John Henry, builder (Manora)	29 Cook Mrs (Parkside)
Neale John Henry (Ferndede)	31 Comber Mrs A.S.
Stephenson Edward (Rose cottage)	33 Hawes, Ernst. Arth (Chaseley)
Miller William (Elm Tree cottage)	35 Oldridge, Jn. (Ferndene)
Ward John C. (Ivy cottage)	37 Harrison Syd.Jas. (Rosecott)
	39 Miller Mrs E. (ElmTreecott)
	41 Vaughan Geo.Wm (Ivy cott)
	43 Hart, Geo. confectioner

Chapel Road
from 51 Commercial Rd only to Church Rd

East Side Kelly's 1918-19	East Side Kelly's 1939
Prospect Place	2 Cooper, Frank
1 Gardiner, William	4 Tenton, Fredk.
2 Arney, Mrs	6 Miller, Jas.
3 Miller, James	8 Bailey, Fredk.Geo
4 Honeybun, Jeffery John	*here is Church Rd*
5 Damon, William	
6 Ballam, J.	
Buckland Cottages	
Marsh, Ch	
Young, Harry	
Inglis, Thomas (Rose Cott)	
Jeffreys, Mrs (Sunnydene)	

Chapel Road
from 51 Commercial Rd only to Church Rd

West Side Kelly's 1918-19	West Side Kelly's 1939
Ponsonby Terrace	3 Mears, Wm
1 Simmonds, Will.Rob	5 Tuppen, Mrs
2 Billett, George	7 Batt Wm.Aubrey
3 Baker, Will.George	9 Damon, Charles
4 Stainer, George	11 Baker, Sidney
5 Stockley, William	13 Giles, Mrs
6 Bourne, John	15 Cattle Mrs
7 Cattle, Edward	19 Plymouth Brethren Meeting Hall
Maidman Ed.C.H. LRIBA architect	
(Westerkirk)	
Parkstone Brotherhood	
Baker, Ch.John (Dane Court Cott)	

Church Crescent (now Church Rd)
from Parr St to Bournemouth Rd

North Side Kelly's 1918-19	North Side Kelly's 1939
Pillar Letter Box	61 Jewer, Jn. (ChurchView)
Hope Cottages	*here is Queen's Grove*
2 Reeves, Miss	55 Brightman, Cyril James
here is Queen's Grove	53 Palmer, Hy.Jas.apartments
1 Bingham, George	51 Horn, Miss L.O. aparts (Bradley)
2 Flower, Willie	49 Piper, F.W. insur.broker
3 Foster, Mrs	49A Ingram, T.K. & Son Ltd florists
4 Horn, Mrs F. apartments	45 Short, Bernard C. (Seafield)
5 Horn, Wallis	41 Wise, Percival A. (St David's)
5 Ingram, Thomas Kendall, florist	*here is Bournemouth Rd*
6 Talbot, Robert	
Ingram, Thomas K. nurseries	
(Portholme)	
Pocock, Misses (St David's)	

<table>
<tr><td colspan="2">

Church Crescent (now Church Rd)
from Parr St to Bournemouth Rd

</td></tr>
</table>

South West Side Kelly's 1918-19	South West Side Kelly's 1939
St Peter's Church	*here is St Peter's road* St Peter's Church *here is Parr Street* 8 Kingston, Leslie Alfd (Homing) 6 Gordon, Mrs (Geneva) 4 Court, Alfd Bayley (Osiris) 4 Court, Miss G. LAM (Eloc) (Osiris) 2 Edwards, Colin (Lewiston Lodge) First Church of Christ Scientist *here is Commercial Road*

<table>
<tr><td colspan="2">

Church Road East (now known as Church Rd)
from Bournemouth Rd to Station Rd

</td></tr>
</table>

East Side Kelly's 1918-19	East Side Kelly's 1939
Carlotta School of Cookery Alton Chambers - Salomon Herman, portrait & miniatrure painter - Holmes, Robert Gabriet Stuart L.D.S.R.C.S. Eng. dental surgeon Julie, Madame, costumier Cathery Fredk. photographer Bedwell G.C. pianoforte dealer Clarke, EdgarEdwin architect & surveyor White, Mrs S. outfitter Wilson A.&F. builders etc (showrooms) Baker, William (South End) Cheshire, George H.J. (Cotgrove) May Mrs (Trentis-Hoe) Edcock John, apartments (Craighurst) Martin Miss E. (Glenthorne) Stuart-Jones Mrs (Timura)	39 Atkins, Miss L. confctnr 37 Gibbs, Miss M 37 Byard A. Geo 37 Finnie Mrs R.H. 35 Williams Miss Gwladys, milliner Julie, Madame costumier 31 Jackson Thos. confnr 29 Parkstone & B'th Co-erative Soc.Ltd 27 The Welric Radio (A.G.Diffey & A.J. Wellman) 25 Sands, F H Statnrs 25 Ponton, Miss W.A.R.C.M. teacher of music 23 Botterill Mrs (South End) 23 Bailey, Miss (South End) 21 Gripper Miss (Leeford) 21 Lathbury Miss (Leeford) 19 Kinchin-Smith Austin Ed. (Little Brampton) 17 Wilson Lt.Col.Thos.O.B.E. (Sharrow) 15 Wood, Wm.J. (The Oaks) 13 Spurr Miss (Trevu) 11 (flat 1) Williams Miss E.A. furrier (Cotgrove) 11 (flat 2) Elliott Mrs (Cotgrove) 9 Tanner, Wm.E. (TrentisHoe) 7 Lever, Miss Florence A.T.C.L.sh. handtypist & languages (Craighurst) 7 Lever Miss L.B. S.R.N., R.F.N,S.C.M. (Craighurst) 7 Vennan, G.J. Ins.broker 5 Lonnen Miss H. (Glenthorne) 3 Moody Jas. (Timaru) 1 Bottomley, Albt.fruiter (LorneHouse) *here is Station Rd*

West Side Kellys 1918-19	
Recreation Grounds	

<table>
<tr><td colspan="2">

Commercial Road
starting with Holly Lodge

</td></tr>
</table>

South Side Kelly's 1918-19	South Side Kelly's 1939
Hudson Mrs (Holly Lodge) Congregational Church Schaub, J.H. (Everley) Geddes Mrs (Cerrito) Tolson Misses (Brandwood) *here is Glenair Rd.* Ure, James Alexander MB surgeon (Glenair) Cross Brothers, builders & undertakers (Pine cott) Moorshead, Thomas Day, Robert, fruiterer *here are Britannia Rd. & Salterns Rd* Potter, Warrie Ch.butcher Prime, H.A. Grocer Wade, Thomas, fruiterer Lush, George William, corn&coal merch Lush, Mrs S. dress makers Guy, Montague Mesher, John fishmonger Leaver, James W Genge, George Wm. butcher Neale, John Hopper Mrs Kilford & Co. bakers&confnrs *here is Curzon Rd* Oak Tree Cottages 1 Pitman, Sidney 2 Baker Fredk.Jn.decorator 3 Phillips, William 4 Holloway, Harry Bacon & Curtis Ltd. wholesale & retail ironmongers *here is Station Rd* Recreation Grounds *here is Church Road east*	12 Hudson Mrs (Holly Lodge) 14 Hants&Dorset Babies'Home(Miss H.S.Heath matron) (Fairholme) Congregational Church 16 Forrest, Francis Penrose M.B.,B.S., M.M.S.A.,F.R.F.R.C.S.Edin.phys& surgeon (Studmore) 16 Barker & Forrest, physcns&surgs (Studmore) 18 Keely Mrs (Cerrito) *here is Glenair Ave.* 24A Cross W.A. builder, san.eng&undertaker 26 B'th & Poole Electricity SupplyCoLtd *here are Britannia and Salterns Rd* 28 Parkington, Fred, fried fish shop 30 Adams, Jas. grocer 32 Elford's florists 34 Viney J.&Sons corn merchs 36 Paddock Mrs C.A. (TheAviary) 38 Mesher & Paddock fishmngrs 38 Paddock, Ernest 44 Neale, John 46 Hopper, Ed.Henry George (Monica) 48 Genge & Young fishmngs *here is Curzon Rd* 50 Williams, Thos. H. 52 Baker, Fredk John 54 Phillips, Miss L.V.M. 56 Mills, Jesse Harry here is Station Rd Parkstone Park *here is Church Road East*

Parkstone Summer Fayre - St Peter's and St Osmund's held on 18th June 1988, Parkstone Green. Church Road shops in background - New Penny Cleaners, Hearing Aid Centre and Herring Estate Agents,

Parkstone Summer Fayre - St Peter's and St Osmund's - held on 18th June 1988, Parkstone Green.
Who is under the disguise?

Commercial Road
starting after North Rd just before Chapel Rd

North Side Kelly's 1918-19	North Side Kelly's 1939
Skerman, E.W. (Monghry)	43 Andrew, Miss Kath.Marg.M.B.Lond,
Broom, James (Parkstone cott)	B.S. phys&med.office Poole
Hatfield, John (Summerland)	Guardian Committee (Parkstone
Payte, Reuben (Tower House)	cott)
Spilsbury, Rob.John (Ponsonby cott)	43 Buckland, Miss H. welfareworker
here is Chapel Rd	R.V. & W.H. Hosp (P'st cott)
Chalkley, John dairyman	45 Payte, Reuben
Wells, Guy, tobacconist	49 Bufton, Leslie W.
Grantham, Ernest Fredk. (SeftonHouse)	49A Draper Mrs K.
Lower, Mrs W.H. (Fairthorne)	49C Wyatt Mrs
Church House	*here is Chapel Rd*
Parkstone School (Rev.E.Stanley Moss	51 Chalkley & Son, dairymen (The
M.A. headmaster)	Hollies)
The Parade	53 Higginson, Jas.David
6 Deayton J. & Son drapers	(MaumburyHo)
4 Rogers, Reginald	55 Turner, Hy.Wm grocer
3 Milne, William, hairdr & tbccnt	57 Sharp, Rev. Canon Arnold Mortimer
2 Flay, C.R. trunk maker	M.A. (rural dean of Poole)
1 Ager, Henry	(Sefton House)
	Parkstone Girls' Grammar School
Central Hotel (Richard Stephenson,	(D'tEdComm) (Prep dept boys & girls 8
propr)	to 10 Miss W.M. Allen M.A.headmistress)
here is Parr Street	69 71 & 73 Deayton's Ltd drapers
Flower A & C drapers	75 Squibb, Wm.Hy.tobccnst
International Tea Co.'s Stores Ltd	75 Cross & French hairdressers
Hicks, John James clothier	77 Flay, Ch.Rob. trunk manufacturer
Staley, Arthur Geo. fruiterer	saddler and sports depot
Parkstone Motor & Cycle Co. cycle	79 Bairtow, Sydney newsagent
dealers	*here is Parr St.*
Green, Geo.Walter baker	83 Carter, Sid football accountant
Wadham-frampton, S.J. butcher	83 Ashley Radio (D.M. Hutchins prop)
Bonnett's Stores, grocers	wireless engineers
Mansell & Co. drapers	87 Vaissiere F.W. clothier
Bennett, George farrier	89 Staley, ARth.Geo. fruiterer
Seller, Arthur Fred. plumber	91 Fraser's Domestic Agency (Mrs A.
Burge, John P. boot maker	Fraser proprietress)
Burge, Mrs Janet, at needlework depot	91B Phillips Mrs W hairdresser
Lanning, Ed & Son fancy bazaar	91C Adams, Rench & Wright Ltd. house
Marston, Henry J. solicitor	& est agents, valuers & insurance
Lawrence, Th.Will.wine & spirit merch	brokers
Malmesbury & Parsons' Dairies Ltd	91C Leeds Provincial Build Society
Loyd W. baker	93A Battrick Freeland Burley
Little, Alf John cycle & motor engineer	93 Green G.W. Ltd bakers
Hebdith, Frank fruiterer	95 Topp & Son butchers
Soul & son butchers	95A Parker Hugh
Carter Mrs A dining rooms	97 & 99 Bonnett's Stores grocers
Allner Albert, builder	101 Genge Mrs N.F. butcher
Woodford Stanley M. registrar of births	103 Turner Mrs N.H. fruiterer
& deaths for the sub dist of Poole	105A Seller A.F.&Sons plumbers
(attends here 2 to 4 pm the 1sts&3rd	107A Reliance Electrical Coelectrs
tuesday ineamnth)	107 Palmer Mrs M.E. art n'dlewkdepot
Fudge, Edwin, Arth. watchmaker	Barnes Miss (Carmel)
Hall A.H.&Sons ironmongers	109 Lanning E.& Son upholsterers
Nat.Prov&UnionBankofEngLtd. (Thos.	111 Ames, Francis Ed.beerretailer &
Fitzroy Blake, mgr)	wine & spirit mer.
Eastman& Son (Dyers&CleanersLtd)	113 Malmesbury & ParsonsDairies Ltd
Dover R.W. tailor (WaterlooHouse)	115 &117 Jelf & Co.motorengineers
Pontifex S.E. (TheOldVicarage)	117 Turner, Mrs
Lloyds Bank Ltd(Wilts&D'tBankbranch)	Soul & Son butchers
(F.W.Harding manager)	123 Carter Mrs A.dining rooms
here are Church Crescent and	125 Allner A. & Sons builders
Springfield Rd	125 Allner Mrs F
	127 Fudge, Edwin Arthur watchmaker
	129 Old, Mrs Hugh, fruiterer
	EnterpriseHardware (W.McEwan)
	131 Nat.Prov.BankLt. (J.Harington
	Barnard, resident manager)
	133 John, EdwardWm. boot repairer
	133A Bollom of Bristol Ltd dyers
	cleaners
	Westminster Bank Ltd
	(RtWarrenSymes,man)
	Symes, Rt.W. (Bankhouse)
	Brixey & Butler, motor garage
	Park Terrace
	1 Maison Vera, ladies hairdres
	2 Nicholson Misses K.& L.M.
	(refrshmntrooms)
	3 Dearnley, A.D.etag & valuer
	4 Elizabeth, gowns & millinery
	5 Pearce A.L. Tobccnst
	6 The Bouquet (Geo Chidwick) frter
	Holmes Rt.Gabriel Stuart L.D.S.R.C.S.Eng
	dentalsurgeon (LloydsBankho)
	141 Lloyds BankLtd
	(K.V.Cowiemanager)
	here are Church Cresc & Springfield Rd

Curzon Road
from Commercial Rd. to Approach Rd.

West Side Kelly's 1918-19	West Side Kelly's 1939
Seller, Arthur Fred (Duneden)	2 Seller, Arth. Fred (Dunedin)
here is Wessex Rd	*here is Wessex Rd*
Little, Mrs W	4 Canning, Jsph.Alex
Lark, Mrs.	6 Shiner Fredk.Geo
Roberts, Henry	8 Coltman, Thomas
Hall, Edward	10 Vivian, Jas
Goulding, Mrs	12 Goulding, Mrs
Pinewood Cottages	14 Rogers, Hubert Edgar
Cookman Miss	16 Carter, Wm.Geo
Carter, William George	18 Way, Fras. Noel
	20 Newman, Harry (The Dell)
Rollings, John	22 Alexander, Thomas (Archwaycott)
Wilson, Montague (The Dell)	
Alexander, Thomas (Archway Cottage)	

Curzon Road
from Commercial Rd. to Approach Rd.

East Side Kelly's 1918-19	East Side Kelly's 1939
Allner, A. builder (works)	Allner A.&Sons, bldrs (works)
Teague, Fredk. (Primrose Cott)	3 Rabbetts, Ernest Wm. (Primrosecott)
Vincent, George (Bushy Cott)	5 Allner, Wm. (Bushy Cott)
White, Charles Henry, sanitary engineer	7 White and Lee, sanitary engineers
(Colthorn)	7 Oates, Hy.Jn.W. (Colthornlodge)
here is Approach Rd	*here is Approach Rd*

Parr Street
from 83 Commercial Rd to Church Rd (1902 map Church St)

West Side Kelly's 1918-19	West Side Kelly's 1939
fr Ashley X to Church Cresc	2 Evans Ernest (Burkden)
Effingham Cottages:	4 McCarthy Mrs
1 Dore, William	6 Dibsdall Mrs E L
2 Haile, John	8 Whitelock,
3 Dibsdall, Fred.Charles	Wilf.Ern.St.Peter'sElem.Schools
4 Diment, Mrs	10 Bull's Head P.M.Mrs Emily
St Peter's Elementary Schools	Augusta Elgar
Seaton, Alb.Hy. beer retailer	*here is St Peter's Rd*
Wicks, Mrs Sarah.shopkeeper	
here is St Peter's Rd	

Salterns Road (previously Marwood Rd)
from Ashley Cross to Rly line

East Side Kelly's 1918-19	East Side Kelly's 1939
Police Station (Frederick Arnold,	1 Gibbs, Bertram
sergeant in charge)	3 Police Station (Wm.Brickell srgeant
Cherrett, Joseph, county constable	in charge)
French, Mrs Annie & son farriers	5 Bealing, Wm.
Laurel Cottages	7 Wilson, Geo.Regd fireman
1 Wilson, George	7A Bennett, Fras farrier
2 Saunders, Charles	Bennett Fras. (Langton)
here is Wessex Rd	9 Crew, Frederick
Wesleyan Methodist Church	11 Guy, Montague Jas
Lawrence, Walter	*here is Wessex Rd*
Lacey, Sydney	Methodist Church
Thorn, William	13 Lawrence Walt.(Gongola)
Palmer, George	15 Lacey Mrs
here is Albert Rd (now Curzon Rd)	17 Thorn Miss (Yatay)
and rly line	19 Frampton, Harry S.B. (St Ivel)
	21 Rogers, Mrs Kate, upholstress
	(HarbourView)
	23 Rogers, K & Son u/takers (Alford)
	here is Curzon Rd and rlyline

Parr Street
from 83 Commercial Rd to Church Rd (1902 map Church St)

East Side Kelly's 1918-19	East Side Kelly's 1939
Tanner, Miss Janet E. Milliner	1 Cox&Dawe confectnrs B'th Markets
Parkstone Motor & Cycle Co. (garage)	Ice & Cold stores Ltd.whol.fruiters
Young, Albert	5 Percy, Hy Jas
Brown, Mrs S.	7 Griffiths, Geo.
Wrann, John	9 Dyke Wltr.Geo.
Norton, Mrs (St Clements)	11 Lacey Jn.Hy
Allen, George William	13 Allen mrs
Hill, Miss Frances, confectnr	15 Holyoak & Everett cnfctners
Oates, Ernest R.	17 Oates Mrs
Guest Buildings:	19 Parkstone Cons.Club (E Towner
Parkstone Conservative & Unionist Club	Hon Sec; Arth.Porter Steward)
(Philip R.Emmott, steward)	21 Wilson K. builder (Alexandraworks)
Wilson, A.&F. builders & contrs.	23 Cull, Mrs
(Alexandra Works)	27 Pollard, Donald L.C.
Telephone Call Office	29 Marsh, Charlie
Wilcox, Joseph hair dresser	31 Beeney, Bernard T. watchmaker
	35 Barrett, Fras.P. ridingmaster
Richards & Lush, jobmasters	37 Lacey, Mrs J. tearooms
Help, George	39 Hall, Fredk.C. bootrepairer
Perris, Josiah, beer retailer	41 Bricklayers' Arms P.H.Arth JRenyard
Rogers, Reginald, furn.dealer	43 Christopher, Mrs L
Talbot, Mrs Alice	45 Burge Miss
Burge, Mrs J	46A Dorset Dairies Direct Milk Supply
Cleall, Fred	Co.Ltd. dairymen (head office)
Saddler, Mrs	49 Lawrence, Mrs E.M.
James, Joseph	51 Gregson, Arthur B.
James, Miss Elsie dressmaker	55 Rickets Mrs
King, Alfred	57 Ward Hy.T. (Holly cottage)
Polden, Mrs Eliza (Ardire)	59 Miller, Geo. Kingswaycott)
	61 Smallwood, George (Kingswaycott)
	63 Renyard Mrs
	65 Polden Mrs Eliza

Salterns Road (previously Marwood Rd)
from Ashley Cross to Rly line

West Side Kelly's 1918-19	West Side Kelly's 1939
Borough of Poole Fire Brigade	here is Britannia Rd
(Parkstone Fire Station) (Capt. W.	Alma Cottages-
Winton, chief officer; James Hardy	1 Cross, Mrs
foreman fireman)	2 Ody, George Alfred
Alma Cottages	4 Talbot, Miss M
1 Oates, Tom	6 Baker, Sidney Wm. chimneysweep
2 Loader, John	8 French, Wm
3 Elton, Reginald	10 Rogers, Chas. shopkeeper
4 Moore, Ernest	12 Turner Mrs
	14 Vivian, Ernest W. (Rylstone)
Randall, Sydney, fried fishshop	16 Saunders Mrs
Rogers, Mrs Emily shopkeeper	18 Allen, David
Turner, Mrs (St. Margaret's)	20 Ellis, Herbt.A. (Montrose)
Hyde, Mrs (Rylstone)	22 Light, Miss (Glenroy)
Ross Cottages	24 Millins, Miss E (Genista)
Saunders, David	26 Fry, Fredk.J. (Hildebert)
Ellis, Alfred	28 Ellis Mrs E.W. (Camville)
	30 Cross, George (Wicklow)
Scrivens, Jas.Wm (Montrose)	32 Whatley, Geo (Ailsa Craig)
Light, Mrs, (Glenroy)	34 Burt, Charles (Olivewood)
Brown, Daniel (Genesta)	36 Primrose, John (Glenwood)
Mastreman Mrs (Hilderbert)	38 Pearce, Arthur, (Homewood)
Ellis, Sydney	here is Tennyson Rd and Rlyline
Cross, George (Wicklow)	
Smith, James (Ailsacraig)	
York Terrace	
1 Holder, Herbert	
2 Primrose, John	
3 Wade, Misses	
4 Pearcy, George	
5 Wright, James	

Station Road
from Commercial Rd to Railway

South Side Kelly's 1918-19	South Side Kelly's 1939
Leverett and Fry grocers	2 Bacon & Curtis Ltd. ironmongers
Cates FJ Library, stationers	4 International Tea Co's Stores Ltd
booksellers etc	6 Brown W.H.&Son, statnrs (Crown
Post T & M.O.O.T.J.Wright postmaster	Library)
(1907 Thos. Lanham PostMaster)	8 Eustace, J.G. Hairdresser
Cartledge, Percy C chemist	8A Christian Science Monitor (The)(Mrs
Hawkes, Joseph Alfred & Son Ltd.	E.E.H. Thompson, representative)
boot & shoe manufacturers	10 Dickson, Thos.G. chemist
Wareham and Dale Ltd butchers	12 Hawkes J.A.&SonLtd.boot and shoe
World's Stores Ltd grocers	manufacturers
Berrill H. hairdresser	14A Cousins&Co. cmmssn.agts.
No 4 Serre, Achille dyers	16A Adams Bros. (Parkstone) Ltd
1, 2 & 3 Jones, Herbert R. draper	wireless engnrs.
here is Wessex Rd.	18 Dover Wm.H. tailor
Haynes Jos.Alfred MPS chemist	20 Wood-Ridley Miss, nurse
Perrett and Batt grocers	20 Fox&Sons, estate agents.
Allen, James Alfred artists colorman	22 Serre Achille Ltd dyers
Sheppard Mrs (Laurel Bank)	Knight Wltr. draper
London & S.W. Railway (Chas.W.	24A Wills Mrs J
Griffiths station master)	26A Moore A.E.
Parkstone Station	26 28&30 Knight Wltr. draper
Telephone Call Box	here is Wessex Rd
Smith WH & Son booksellers and	32 Savill Alfd.&Sons F.L.A.S. F.S.I.
newsagents (bookstall L & SWR)	surveyors
Parkstone Hotel Frederick Foddy	32 Guest Consolidated Estates
Corbin Richard Elliott	Haynes Jsph.Alfd.pharmacist (ParkView)
	34 Perrett & Batt, grocers
	36 Noble Percy B. tobccnst
	Parkstone Motor Co.Ltd. (garage)
	Hine Mrs (Laurel Bank)
	Benham A. (Dawn)
	Scrivens Frank, furnituremover
	(Home) Teleohone, Parkstone 729
	Cull Mrs (Dinton)
	Allsopp Miss J. (Jaminecott)
	Morgan Mrs (Ty-Bryn)
	Harper Wm. (Ivydene)
	Southern Railway (London&South
	Western section).(Chas.Saunders,station
	master) (Parkstonestation) (1907 Henry
	Hills station master)
	Smith W.H.&SonLtd.booksllrs.
	(bookstall, Southern Railway)
	Parkstone Station Hotel (Mr & Mrs
	Gerald Cogdale)
	Corbin Mrs (Wellington)
	Corbin and Deacon, plumbers
	Deacon Harry (Greystones)

Old photograph of Station Road at its junction with Commercial Road. From left: Hawkes Shoes, Chemist (probably Cartledge), the Post Office, (now Wessex Needlecraft), Hunts Library (now Crown Corner Newsagents), Leverett & Frye (now Fishmaster).
Courtesy: Mrs Janet Fox

Station Road
from Commercial Rd to railway

North Side Kelly's 1918-19	North Side Kelly's 1939
Parkstone Park	Parkstone Park
Station Corner Chambers -	*here is Church Rd*
Rumsey&Rumsey Auctioneers	Rumsey&Rumsey F.A.I. auctioneers est
Adkins L. (Crawford)	agents, surveyors&valuers
James & Sons auctioneers & est ag.	Blott Thos.Geo (Crawford)
The Hamworthy Clay Co. clay	IsleofThanet Building Society
contractors	(James&Sons) district office
Hewett and Hewett tailors	James and Sons, auctioneers
Rae Capt. (The Limes)	Hewett and Hewett tailors
	Walters Miss E (One Aye)
	Craster Mrs (Lime Treecot)
	here is Ardmore Rd

Wessex Road
from 30 Station Rd to Salterns Rd

South Side Kelly's 1918-19	South Side Kelly's 1939
here is Approach Rd	*here is Approach Rd*
Partridge, Saml.J. (Glenside)	30　Eyres Geo
Rabbetts, Gilbert C.	30　Eyres G&Son chimneysweeps
Towner, Edward David (The Glen)	28　Patrick, Fredk.G. (TheGlen)
Schoales, Wilfred (Melbourne)	26　Guest, Fras.Ivor
Gallop, Wm.Jas (Sydenham)	26B Webb, Mrs
Coles, John S. coal merchant	22　Gallop, Wm.Js (Sydenham)
James, Frederick (Glencairn)	20　Dean, Wilfred
Rabbits, Mrs J. (Rosario)	18　Allner Geo. (Glencairn)
Lanning, Mrs H. (The Laurels)	Allner A&Sons.bldrs (Glencairn)
here is Curzon Rd	16　Rabbetts, Aubrey (Rosario)
Rose Cottages	14　Whittaker L.C. (The Laurels)
Earney, George	*here is Curzon Rd*
Adams Miss	12　Earney, Mrs (Rose cot)
	10　Northeast, Harold Jas
	8　Skinner, Hy
	6　Vivian Miss (Ross-Dhu)
	4　Withers, Raymond
	2　Russell Fredk.Chas
	Methodist Church

Wessex Road
from 30 Station Rd to Salterns Rd

North Side Kelly's 1918-19	North Side Kelly's 1939
Toms, John (Ivy Cottage)	Frizzell, Percy, signwriter (works)
Gale, William (Fern Cottage)	Berriman, Godfrey, bldr
Myrtle Cottages	St.John AmbulanceBrigade, PooleCorps
2　Parker, Mrs	(E.Paddock corps sec) headquarters
1　Rooker, Charles	7　Needham, E.H. (Fern cott)
	5　Dyson, Ernest H. (Ivycott)
	3　Dawe, Victor Wm
	1　Rooker Mrs

**Commercial Road, looking towards Poole, before road
widening in 1961.** Bonnett's Stores on right is now Viney's
Garden Centre.
Courtesy: Mr J E Paddock

■ *Current Shops as in December 1995*

Commercial Road
The Parade

North Side
Current shops, as in
December 1995

Worldwide Boat Service Ltd
Janson Press 71
La Brasserie Restaurant
Mandarin Chef Take Away
New Mandarin Chef Chinese Restaurant
Central Hotel corner with Parr Street
East corner with Parr Street - Edwards
florist & Perrins Guy Williams solicitors
above
Christian Science Reading Rooms
Empty
Empty
The Rock Shop
Sheila Hearn, hairdresser 85
Acorn Graphics
Empty
Vineys
Royal Liver Insurance
Empty
Poole Instant Print
Spar mini-market
Poole Ski/windsurfer Centre 111
here is alleyway - Old Parkstone Dairy at
back
Aspray est agents
Top Man gents hairdresser
Harrison Robertshaw est agents
Scrumps sandwich bar
The Village Barber (Park View House
123)
Poppy Designs curtains and blinds
Knightstone Housing Association
Empty
Radio House
Golf Shop
Michael B ladies hairdresser
Oxfam
David Moore ladies hairdresser
Latinis Restaurant (previously Sunnyside
Restaurant for 30 years, Mr & Mrs Folkes)
Fox & Sons est agents
Lawtons News
Mutiara Malaysian & Chinese Cuisine
(previously Cherries and The Bouquet)
Lloyds Bank
here is Church Road/Springfield Road

Commercial Road
Corner with Britannia Road - Briggs
House - Executive Homes est agents
& Ashley Business Centre

South Side
Current shops, as in
December 1995

here is Salterns Road
here is Curzon Road
Fabric Warehouse
Wolfpack Trading Post
The Gate of India Restaurant
A Plan Insurance

Bournemouth Road

North Side
Current shops, as in
December 1995

here is Springfield Road
Midland Bank
Mews Funeral directors
Wilson Thomas est agents
Pamela Louise Ladies fashions
Barclays Bank
Bristol and West Building Society
Blacklock chemist
Kitchen Elegance 19
Parkstone Park Wines off licence 21
Empty
Mace mini-market
Parkstone Post Office

Church Road
overlooking Parkstone Park

East Side
Current shops, as in
December 1995

Herring Bowman est agents
Alton Chambers 37 J M Fairhall, solicitors
SSAFA charity shop
Noah's Pet Shop
Parkstone Craft Galleries
Pooleline Systems
Strides Dry Cleaners
Hearing Aid Centre
Herring est agents

Station Road
from Commercial Road

Current shops, as in
December 1995

Empty
Fishmaster
Crown Corner newsagents
Wessex Needlecraft Mrs Janet Fox (this
was the old Parkstone Post Office)
Park Pharmacy 10 Mr Ritchie
Hawkes Shoes (believed to date back to
early 1900's)
Empty
Empty
Reptiles Plus
Cox Tredrea Solicitors
Empty
Fleur de Lys florist
John Neame Swimming Pools (was
Knights drapers for several decades)
here is Wessex Road and Approach Road
- on corner The Dorset Natural Health
Centre
Isabel's Restaurant (previousl A J Haynes
chemist)
Parkstone Outdoor Adventure Clothing
(once Perrett's Stores, grocer)
Homelake House (once Parkstone Motor
Company)
Further up is Parkstone Railway Station
and Parkstone Hotel.

Index

Index continued on page 64...

Congregational Church Young People's Club.
Drama Section. Date: Probably early 1950's.
Courtesy: Mrs Edna Dickinson

Gran and Grandad Cadman with delivery horse and cart -
1907 at 14 Britannia Road.
Courtesy: the late Mrs Kath Raymond.

Cadman Family Photo c 1914.
Standing from left: Ethel Audrey Teague, Emily Amelia Teague,
Fred Teague and Jim Teague. Seated from left: George Teague
born on Brownsea Island, Horace Shadrack Teague and Gran
Cadman (Ellen Elizabeth Teague).
Courtesy the late Mrs Kath Raymond.

A Postcard from Reverend Willoughby Gee
Courtesy: Mrs Edna Dickinson

Acknowledgements

Without the help of these and many other people, there would not have been a book on Ashley Cross and I am grateful for their time and efforts. If I have missed out anyone, please accept my apologies:-

Mr Donald Adams, Mrs Hazel Boyd, Mr George Chidwick, Mr Colin Dean,
Miss Iris Evernden, Mr Denis Gooding, Mr B Grant-Braham, Mrs Barbara Handscombe,
Maureen and Leslie Keats, Mrs Barbara Langley, Reverend Nigel Lloyd, Mr Christopher Luxford,
Reverend Margaret Mulraine, Reverend Diana Newman, Mrs Elsie Murray, Mrs Marie Parkins,
Mr Douglas Pike, Mrs Iris Ringrow of St John Ambulance, Mrs Rachel Shering, the late Mrs Kath
Symonds, Mr David Tremain, Mrs Doreen Viney, Mrs Marion Watson, Mr Alex Wilson.